NORITO

NORITO

**A Translation of the Ancient
Japanese Ritual Prayers**

by

Donald L. Philippi

With a new Preface by
Joseph M. Kitagawa

PRINCETON UNIVERSITY PRESS
PRINCETON, NEW JERSEY

COPYRIGHT © 1990 BY PRINCETON UNIVERSITY PRESS

PUBLISHED BY PRINCETON UNIVERSITY PRESS, 41 WILLIAM STREET,

PRINCETON, NEW JERSEY 08540

IN THE UNITED KINGDOM: PRINCETON UNIVERSITY PRESS, OXFORD

LIBRARY OF CONGRESS CATALOGING-IN-PUBLICATION DATA

ENGISHIKI NORITO. ENGLISH.

NORITO: A TRANSLATION OF THE ANCIENT JAPANESE RITUAL PRAYERS / BY

DONALD L. PHILIPPI.

P. CM.

TRANSLATION OF: ENGISHIKI NORITO.

INCLUDES BIBLIOGRAPHICAL REFERENCES.

ISBN 0-691-06859-3 (ACID-FREE PAPER)

ISBN 0-691-01489-2 (PBK. : ACID-FREE PAPER)

1. SHINTO—PRAYER-BOOKS AND DEVOTIONS—ENGLISH. I. PHILIPPI,

DONALD L. II. TITLE.

BL2224.3.E5413   1990

299'.56138—DC20   90-8231

THIS BOOK HAS BEEN COMPOSED IN TIMES ROMAN

PRINCETON UNIVERSITY PRESS BOOKS ARE PRINTED ON ACID-FREE PAPER, AND
MEET THE GUIDELINES FOR PERMANENCE AND DURABILITY OF THE COMMITTEE
ON PRODUCTION GUIDELINES FOR BOOK LONGEVITY OF THE COUNCIL ON

LIBRARY RESOURCES

PRINTED IN THE UNITED STATES OF AMERICA

BY PRINCETON UNIVERSITY PRESS

PRINCETON, NEW JERSEY

10 9 8 7 6 5 4 3 2 1

(PBK.) 10 9 8 7 6 5 4 3 2 1

ORIGINALLY PUBLISHED BY THE INSTITUTE FOR JAPANESE CULTURE
AND CLASSICS, KOKUGAKUIN UNIVERSITY, TOKYO, 1959

CONTENTS

PREFACE

Joseph M. Kitagawa

This preface is meant to elucidate the not-so-readily apparent significance of *norito*, the ancient Japanese ritual prayers, with reference to Donald L. Philippi's small but well-researched, creative, and innovative volume on the subject. Invariably our account, like all discussions of non-Western traditions, is compelled to begin with the historic encounter between East and West.

THE "STRANGENESS" OF NON-WESTERN TRADITIONS

Those who remember the days prior to World War II tell us how little the West then knew about the non-Western world. This was true even in America, which had been developing into a full-fledged Pacific power since the latter part of the nineteenth century.[1] As we look back it becomes evident, however, that World War II made a tremendous difference in Americans' as well as in other Westerners' familiarity with things non-Western. Here in America, particularly, the national emergency required training and instructional programs in Asian subjects, and there appeared an amazing array of books and articles on Asia, from the very scholarly to the ridiculous.[2]

Further, the newly aroused interest in Asia among Americans and other Westerners did not diminish at the end of the Pacific war. In fact it has grown steadily for the past thirty years, as exemplified by the phenomenal increase in Asian and other non-Western studies in various Western educational institutions. Over time, the interest in things non-Western became no longer confined to colleges and universities. To be sure, the "Orient" (as the East used to be referred to) always had an aura of mystery for a small number of Western minds, primarily symbolizing—to borrow Arthur Christy's expression—

---

1) Meribeth E. Cameron once quipped that before the war "few Americans could name any Asiatics except Confucius, Gandhi, and Chiang Kai-shek." According to Harold Isaacs, more than 40 percent of the American population in 1942 could not locate India or China on a map. And in 1945, after three years of American direct military involvement in Asia, only 43 and 45 percent of the American populace could locate the countries, respectively. Harold Isaacs, *Scratches on the Mind* (New York: John Day, 1959), p. 39.

2) See Meribeth E. Cameron, "Far Eastern Studies in the U.S.," *The Far Eastern Quarterly* 12, no. 2 (February 1948): 119–20.

something "far away and long ago."[3] In our time, however, we find a vastly different situation: Many Western people, for example, have come into direct contact with Japan, resulting in an increasing familiarity with Japanese art, literature, cuisine, and cinema, as well as with karate, judo, Zen meditation, and Japanese-manufactured automobiles, television sets, and videocassette recorders.

Such a rapid growth in Westerners' interests in things non-Western and the concomitant increase in travel and dialogue between the Western and Eastern cultures are impressive, but there is much truth in Mircea Eliade's astute and sobering observation that:

> most of the time, [our] encounters and comparisons with non-Western cultures have not made all the "strangeness" of these cultures evident. . . . This is due to the fact that the encounters have been made through their more Westernized representatives, or in the mainly external spheres of economics or politics. We may say that *the Western world has not yet, or not generally, met with authentic representatives of the "real" non-Western traditions.*[4]

Eliade's observation is a fair warning as we confront the strangeness of *norito*, the ancient Japanese form of ritual prayers, and itself assuredly one of the authentic foreign representatives in Eliade's sense.

"MAN'S WESTERN QUEST"

To further complicate the matter of dialogue between Western and non-Western cultures, there is today a peculiar belief among some modern Western scholars and some Western-inspired young Asian scholars alike that they have already discovered the correct approaches to unfolding the mystery of the historical-cultural destiny of the entire human race. In fact, they are totally oblivious to the "strangeness" of some traditions, the strangeness that is necessarily inherent in things truly "other," or the "authentic representatives" in Eliade's terms. These scholars are overconfident that the approaches, perspectives, and methods they use are the most dependable and trustworthy tools for dealing with different linguistic, social, cultural, and religious traditions in all

---

3) Arthur E. Christy, ed., *The Asian Legacy and American Life* (New York: John Day, 1942), pp. 1–55.

4) Mircea Eliade, *Myths, Dreams and Mysteries*, trans. P. Mariet (New York: Harper, 1960), pp. 8–9. My italics.

parts of the world. But these tools have a history of their own, having been developed within a Western tradition that has always attempted to integrate and interfuse all the disparate strands of human civilization into its own *mundus imaginalis*. It may therefore be worth reviewing briefly the intellectual heritage of what Denis de Rougemont calls "Man's Western Quest."[5]

In a sense, "Man's Western Quest" can be traced all the way back to the ancient Greek notion of "system," which, as Betty Heimann has cogently pointed out, implied composition in a rational order, based on a postulate that the human mind thinks systematically. No wonder Protagoras maintained that "man is the measure of all things."[6] In the course of time, the Greek characterization of humanity was infused with the Hebrew-Christian concept of *imago dei*, and it was exposed to the Persian Zoroastrian theory of the "end of the world" (*eschaton*), itself mediated by the Jewish and Christian traditions.

In this connection, it is worth mentioning that the Western notion of *anthropos* always tended to lean toward the idea of "progress," a word derived from the Latin term *gressus*, or "step," which suggests the act of stepping forward. "Progress" was a theoretically abstract *concept* that became transformed into an *idea* of progress, as Paul Tillich has reminded us; indeed, the *idea* of progress is more an interpretation of an actual historical situation in terms of the *concept* of progress:

> There is a difference between the concept of progress and the idea of progress. The concept of progress is an abstraction, based on the description of a group of facts, of objects of observation which may well be verified or falsified; but the idea of progress is an interpretation of existence as a whole, which means first of all our own existence.[7]

Actually, Western intellectual history serves as a good illustration of how easily the *concept* of progress can be metamorphosed into the *idea* of progress, which in turn can become a *doctrine* of the law of history, or even an unconscious *dogma* of progressiveness. It is equally significant that the Western sense of history came to be amplified by a self-authenticating circular religious logic, especially after the Christian tradition became the state religion of the Roman empire in the fourth century.

---

5) See Denis de Rougemont, *Man's Western Quest* (Westport, Conn.: Greenwood, 1973).
6) Betty Heimann, *Indian and Western Philosophy: A Study in Contrast* (London: G. Allen & Unwin, 1937), pp. 27–28.
7) Paul Tillich, *The Future of Religions*, ed. J. C. Brauer (New York: Harper, 1966), p. 64.

Apparently, the Western tradition regarded it a sign of its own progress to encounter, and eventually absorb into its own framework, many different features of human civilization, especially during the Christian-dominated religious/cultural/social/political synthesis in medieval Europe.[8] It is well known that medieval European civilization revolved around three pivotal institutions—the Church (*sacerdotium*), the state (*imperium*), and the university (*studium*). And, as might be expected, many Europeans came to be convinced that their synthesis was the most advanced and progressive in the world, because their tradition was given "cosmic legitimation" by Christianity, following the self-authenticating circular logic of its religious rhetoric.

From the perspective of ecclesiastical Christian logic, Judaism after the coming of Christ was no longer an authentic divine religion since the ancient Hebrew tradition had been fulfilled by the birth of Christianity. In a similar vein, many Europeans identified Mohammed as the false prophet in the Johannine apocalypse and thus regarded Islam as a false and misguided faith. Ironically, it was from Muslims and Jews in Spain that the Christian world learned philosophy, especially Greek philosophy, thereby benefiting both Christian Scholasticism and the medieval European university. It is pertinent, too, to remember that it was the Spaniards and the Portuguese who, having been heavily influenced by Islam (the this-worldly religion par excellence), initiated in the non-Christian world the wave of European colonialism and Christian missionary work that began almost immediately after the celebrated voyages of Christopher Columbus and Vasco da Gama.

THE QUESTIONABLE OBJECTIVITY OF THE CONTEMPORARY CRITICAL METHOD

In retrospect, it becomes evident that during the past five centuries the intellectual topography of Europe has undergone many significant changes inspired by, among other movements and events, the Renaissance, the Reformation, nationalism, the Industrial Revolution, and the French Revolution. It is often said that the Renaissance, by bringing down the center of gravity of the world from heaven to earth, gave birth to the new conception of civilization, that is, Western civilization as a pseudo-religion of secularized salvation. Rejecting the thesis of the *corpus Christianum* that civilization was to be

---

8) See Bryan Wilson, *Contemporary Transformations of Religion* (Oxford: Clarendon, 1976), pp. 9–10.

guided by ecclesiastical authority, modern Europeans came to regard themselves as the inventors and transmitters of true civilization. Moreover, during the Enlightenment of the eighteenth century, intellectuals made another cognitive somersault, whereby various fields of knowledge formerly circumscribed in the university by the domains of metaphysics and theology were liberated. In the words of Ernst Cassirer:

> They no longer look to the concept of God for their justification and legitimation; the various sciences themselves now determine the concept on the basis of their specific form. The relations between the concept of God and the concepts of truth, morality, [and] law are by no means abandoned, but their directions change.[9]

In this connection, it should be noted that the Christian missionary enterprise in Asia and Africa during the nineteenth century cooperated, unwittingly or otherwise, with European colonialism, and this cooperation led to Christianity's coming to be viewed by outsiders as an important ingredient of Western civilization. And the combined forces of Western civilization, Christian missionary programs, and colonial expansion brought about social, political, economic, cultural, and religious changes in much of the non-Western world by the end of the nineteenth century.

This is neither the time nor the place to discuss the merits and demerits of colonialism. However, it is worth quoting an Indian thinker, Ashis Nandy, who commented on colonialism from the perspective of those who were once "governed" by a foreign colonial administration. According to Nandy:

> Modern colonialism won its great victories not so much through its military and technological prowess as its ability to create secular hierarchies incompatible with the traditional order [in the non-Western world]. These hierarchies opened up new vistas for many, particularly for those exploited or cornered within the traditional order. To them the new order looked like—and here lay its psychological pull—the first step towards a more just and equal world. That was why some of the finest minds in Europe—and in the East—were to feel that colonialism . . . would open up the non-West to the modern critical-analytic spirit. . . . It would be critical in the sense in which the Western tradition of social criticism—

9) Ernst Cassirer, *The Philosophy of the Enlightenment* (Princeton: Princeton University Press, 1950), p. 159.

from Vico to Marx—had been critical and it would be rational in the sense in which post-Cartesian Europe had been rational.[10]

In addition to the new secular hierarchy described by Nandy, other attributes claimed by the West, such as objectivity, neutrality, and universality (science); global capitalism (commerce); eternal truth (religion); the psychic unity of humankind (social sciences);[11] and totality (Marxism),[12] had their respective followers in the East. Underlying all these different claims of the modern West was the daring thesis, articulated by Hegel, that Western thought (no longer simply "man," as in Protagoras's formulation) was the "measure of all things."[13]

It is important for us to understand Hegel's thinking, because his ghost is still very much alive among contemporary scholars, not only in the West but also in the non-Western world among Western-inspired thinkers (philosophers, scientists, humanists, Marxists, religious thinkers, etc.). It was Hegel who asserted that "the 'phenomenology' or self-manifestation merges into man's work in history, into human self-fulfillment. Man becomes 'present God' (*präsenter Gott*) and continues the divine process in his own worldly presence."[14] In his scheme of the history of philosophy, Hegel was convinced that "the Occident supersedes the Orient, and in dealing with the Oriental traditions, it faces, in a sense, its own petrified past."[15]

During the nineteenth century, and even in the twentieth century up to World War II, under the strong impact of the Westernization of the whole world, many Asian thinkers accepted the West's questionable and self-authenticating claim that "Asian thought is comprehensible and interpretable within European thought, but not vice versa. . . . *European thought has to provide the context and categories* for the exploration of all traditions of thought."[16] One cannot simply be amused by such Europo-centric views of the last cen-

---

10) Ashis Nandy, *The Intimate Enemy: Loss and Recovery of Self under Colonialism* (Delhi: Oxford University Press, 1983), p. ix.

11) See Klaus-Peter Koepping, *Adolf Bastian and the Psychic Unity of Mankind* (St. Lucia: University of Queensland Press, 1983).

12) See Martin Jay, *Marxism and Totality* (Berkeley: University of California Press, 1984).

13) See Wilhelm Halbfass, *India and Europe* (Albany: SUNY Press, 1988), p. 84.

14) Ibid., p. 93.

15) Ibid., p. 88.

16) Ibid., p. 96. My italics.

tury, for an amazing number of Western Orientalists even today take for granted E. Husserl's judgment that:

> Europe alone can provide other traditions with a *universal framework of meaning and understanding*. They will have to "Europeanize themselves, whereas we . . . will never, for example, Indianize ourselves." The "Europeanization of all foreign parts of mankind" . . . is the destiny of the earth.[17]

Happily, today, there are thinkers and scholars (still few in number but increasing steadily) both in the West and in the non-Western world who reject Husserl's simplistic thesis that the Europeanization of the entire world is the destiny of the earth, and who realize that the Western-inspired scholarly approach may not be as objective, neutral, or universal as many of us have been led to believe for so long. They recognize only too well that much of the contemporary critical, rationalistic, and analytical approaches, which are taken for granted in humanistic, scientific, and social scientific studies, are based on the peculiar Western convention of dividing human experience into semi-autonomous pigeonholes, such as religion, philosophy, ethics, aesthetics, culture, and society. Obviously, this type of convention is useful within a specified discourse, affirmed "autobiographically" by people within the Western tradition as sort of a family language. However, some continue to feel that it has universal validity, partly because these provincial people are not aware of other—specifically, in our context, non-Western—ways of discerning the texture of human experience.

Actually, people everywhere, including those in the West, live and breathe in their respective seamless whole—what, in effect, is a synthesis of religious, cultural, social, economic, and political orders, to use the Western convention of divided categories. Many astute scholars and thinkers in both the West and the East are now persuaded that useful though Western-inspired methodology may be, it is based on a particular, provincial taxonomy and cannot be employed indiscriminately in what amounts to a cookie-cutter approach to analyzing non-Western traditions. For example, in the Western idiom we designate "religion" as its own, autonomous category; however, this designation is beginning to be questioned as we realize that religion is integrated in a sys-

---

17) Quoted in ibid., p. 437. My italics.

tem, providing "cosmic legitimation" to each synthesis. Apropos of this realization, the sensitive Islamicist Bernard Lewis recently wrote:

> When we in the Western world, nurtured in the Western tradition, use the words "Islam" and "Islamic," we tend to make a natural error and assume that the religion means the same for Muslims as it has meant in the Western world . . . that is to say, a section or compartment of life reserved for certain matters, and separate, or at least separable, from other compartments of life designed to hold other matters.[18]

Similarly, the ancient Japanese religion, which was based on particular Japanese conventions and ways of thinking for perceiving the kinds and levels of reality, cannot be studied simply by means of our usual critical-analytical methods, as Donald Philippi cogently demonstrates in his perceptive study of *norito*.

MIXED LEGACIES OF MODERN JAPANESE LINGUISTIC AND THOUGHT FORMS

In studying any aspect of non-Western traditions, it is customary to stress the importance of sufficient familiarity with the foreign languages involved. This exhortation assumes that our knowledge of a particular native language will give us entrée into the art, literature, and philosophy of the culture in which it is spoken. It must be perplexing, therefore, to find that our acquaintance with modern Japanese linguistic and thought forms, imperative though that familiarity is, may not really provide us with the level and kind of access to the meanings of Japanese traditions—ancient through pre-modern—as we expect them to unfold within a particular set of historical circumstances. To be sure, many people today in Japan and elsewhere, especially in the West, are totally oblivious to or unconcerned with this dilemma; however, unlike those who are interested primarily in contemporary economics, politics, or sociology (and who can thus sidestep to a great extent this particular kind of quandary), those who attempt to capture the meaning of ancient Japanese religion—or of *norito*, for that matter—can ill afford to ignore this bewildering problem.

---

18) Bernard Lewis, *The Political Language of Islam* (Chicago: The University of Chicago Press, 1988), p. 2.

Considering the importance of the linguistic and thought forms involved, it might be useful and necessary for us to make a short detour and discuss what happened to Japanese language and thought systems in the modern world. To the Japanese, 1868 was a significant date, for in the previous year the exhausted and fatigued Tokugawa feudal regime (*bakufu* or *shōgunate*), which had ruled Japan since 1603, surrendered its prerogative to the teenaged emperor, Meiji; this turn of events precipitated the resumption of imperial rule, though Japan was actually being governed by a group of pragmatic-minded advisers. Curiously, the new imperial regime had two diametrically opposed "faces": 1) *ōsei fukko* ("restoration of monarchical rule"), implying a return to the *old* polity of the Ritsuryō ("imperial edict") system of the seventh and eighth centuries (and thus relevant to our discussions of ancient Japanese religion and *norito*), and 2) *ishin* ("renovation"), which represented the entering into a *new* chapter in history. The inevitable tension between these two faces may account for much of the existential contradictions, stresses, and strains of modern Japan.

In modern Japan, that which was "old" was not exclusively defined by its opposition to that which was "new"; similarly, the "new" did not connote an intrinsic rupture with the "old." For example, the Meiji regime elevated the throne in the manner of the ancient Ritsuryō polity, but it rejected other Ritsuryō principles, such as that of mutual dependence between the sovereign's and the Buddha's laws (*ōbō-Buppō*). Accordingly, the Meiji government legally separated Shinto and Buddhism, signifying a sudden undoing by fiat of the historical pattern of a Shinto-Buddhist amalgam (*Shin-Butsu shūgō*). Clearly, the new government wished to depend only on the native Shinto to provide it with "cosmic legitimation." On the other hand, the regime was aware of being in a tight spot with regard to its anti-Christian policy, a legacy of the Tokugawa *shōgunate*. And, mostly because the Japanese government was determined to rectify the unequal clauses in its treaties with the Western powers (who took a dim view of the Japanese anti-Christian policy), the government lifted the ban against Christianity, thus allowing its people a token form of religious liberty.

It is evident that the Meiji regime wanted to maintain Japan's political independence at a time when much of the non-Western world was being swallowed up by European colonialism. Confronted with the powerful West, Japanese leaders resorted to a compromise formula, "Eastern Ethics and Western

Learning-Technology" (*Tōyō no Dōtoku, Seiyō no Gakugei*),[19] reflecting their double-edged intention of welcoming and utilizing "Western know-how," precisely for the purpose of keeping the West at arm's length, while relying on traditional "Eastern Ethics" to consolidate the Japanese nation inwardly. In the course of time, Japan came to emulate Western-style colonialism and aspired to become the leading "imperial power" in East Asia (*Tōyō no Meishu*). This intriguing political development had direct bearing on the linguistic and thought forms that are problematic for us now.

Opinions vary widely on the question of whether the Meiji leaders realized all the ramifications of their undertaking to import features of Western civilization, even if these were meant to serve only as "practical means." A young Meiji emperor proclaimed as a Charter Oath, "Knowledge and learning shall be sought throughout the world."[20] But this was far easier said than done; modern Japanese people encountered a series of almost insurmountable hurdles, starting with linguistic problems. In a way, modern Japan's linguistic problem recalls the Japanese experience during the fifth and sixth centuries A.D., when Sino-Korean civilization penetrated preliterate Japan. That encounter also resulted in a serious linguistic predicament: the effort to adapt characters of a monosyllabic language such as Chinese to the polysyllabic Japanese language. In time, the Japanese developed an ingenious, though very cumbersome, hybrid linguistic device, commonly referred to as the *wa-kan* ("Japanese-Chinese") style, which served to mediate, amazingly successfully, alien Chinese and Buddhist idioms, concepts, poems, literary works, arts, logic, and rhetoric to the Japanese mind.[21] It is an irony of history that in the second half of the nineteenth century Japan had to confront yet another alien civilization—Western—embodied in various linguistic systems, for example, English, German, French, and Dutch. And what developed out of this new round of encounters with a foreign civilization was another kind of mixture, *wa-yō setchū*, a form of Japanese (involving the *wa-kan* hybrid system) and Western blending, which spawned the phenomenon of *wakon yōsai* ("a Japanese spirit with foreign abilities").

---

19) Tsunoda Ryūsaku et al., comps., *Sources of Japanese Tradition* (New York: Columbia University Press, 1958), pp. 603–8.

20) On "Charter Oaths," see G. B. Sansom, *The Western World and Japan* (New York: A. A. Knopf, 1949), pp. 318–20.

21) Both the advantages and the disadvantages of the *wa-kan* device are ably discussed in David Pollack, *The Fracture of Meaning: Japan's Synthesis of China from the Eighth through the Eighteenth Centuries* (Princeton: Princeton University Press, 1986).

We must bear in mind that Western civilization reached its zenith during the nineteenth century, and some people even speculated that the East would soon be absorbed by the West. In that kind of atmosphere, the West's somewhat exaggerated claim to superiority and universality was bought on face value by some non-Western, including Japanese, leaders. After all, Hegel, who had become an idol of Japanese intellectuals, asserted with utter seriousness that in comparing and evaluating various cultural traditions "the course of history itself" decided in favor of the European tradition.[22] It was not surprising, therefore, that numerous new words, concepts, idioms, and symbols penetrated Japan from the allegedly "superior and universalistic" Western civilization. It should be noted that this trend meant more than just the introduction of new words and expressions. As S. Ichikawa astutely observed, "even the structure of the Japanese language" itself was destined to be greatly modified.[23] In that kind of climate, there were not enough people who were reflective and critical, not only about the differences between Western and Japanese languages, but also, and more important, about the different conventions employed by Westerners and the Japanese in their perceptions of the textures of human experience.

This lack of analysis was due partly to the fact that those who were familiar with the inherited Japanese tradition generally were not exposed to Western languages and thought, whereas the iconoclastic youths (somewhat analogous to those who, "exploited or cornered within the traditional order," as Ashis Nandy noted, welcomed new secular hierarchies in the non-Western world) were willing to accept Western experience as the paradigm for new Japan.

The vogue for things Western in Japan during the latter part of the nineteenth century—stimulated partly by the pragmatic Meiji regime's promotion of "Westernism," ostensibly to improve Japan's standing in its treaties with Western powers—coincided with the impressive growth of Western-oriented Japanology. It should be noted that the Japanology in question was a variation on what was usually called in the West a discipline that examined various facets of Eastern peoples—their languages, arts, economic systems, social and political orders, religions, and cultures—and yields "data" that were then subjected to scholarly analysis and interpretation based on "Western"

---

22) See nn. 13, 14, and 15, above.
23) See S. Ichikawa, "Foreign Influence in the Japanese Language," in I. Nitobe et al., *Western Influences in Modern Japan* (Chicago: The University of Chicago Press, 1931), pp. 141–80.

models, concepts, and logic. This type of Western-oriented Japanology was promoted by the Asiatic Society of Japan (ASJ), which began its activities as early as 1872. As might be expected, most of the famous Western Japanologists, as well as some Japanese scholars familiar with Western Japanology, were active in the ASJ, and they made pioneering contributions to the study of various aspects of Japanese tradition.[24]

Even with due recognition of the numerous positive aspects resulting from the strong impact of Western civilization on modern Japan, we should not ignore some of the negative features. On this score, it is not unreasonable to ask whether the Japanology that emerged in the late nineteenth century and the modern Japanese linguistic and thought systems (heavily modified under the impact of Western civilization), both of which were rooted in the provincial Western convention of dividing human experience into a particular series of autonomous compartments (as well as in notions of *anthropos* and history), can adequately reveal the meanings of ancient or pre-modern Japanese traditions. Do they, unconsciously to be sure, superimpose Western concepts and logic on Japanese traditions, whereby data about ancient or medieval Japan become ingredients to be analyzed by and potentially absorbed into what Hegel and Husserl regarded as the only world civilization, the *telos* of which is to be determined exclusively by the West? The question might also be asked whether Japanese tradition, before it came under the powerful influence of the West, possessed a worthwhile system of meaning that was an alternative to that of the Europocentric modern world. Or could the encounter and dialogue between cultures—Western versus pre-modern or modern Japanese, for example—take place only "*in* a Westernized world, under conditions shaped by Western ways of thinking?"[25]

Since the end of World War II, these have become very pertinent questions in Japan with regard to our understanding and interpretation of various facets of the historical Japanese tradition. For, living as we do in the latter part of the twentieth century, we often forget the decisive importance of 1945, that it represents a dividing line between two different worlds of experience for the

24) See Joseph M. Kitagawa, "Some Reflections on Foreign Scholars' Understanding of Japanese Culture and Shinto," which originally appeared in *Proceedings of the Second International Conference for Shinto Studies* (Tokyo: Kokugakuin University, 1968), pp. 122–34; included in Kitagawa, *On Understanding Japanese Religion* (Princeton: Princeton University Press, 1987), pp. 286–96.
25) Halbfass, *India and Europe*, p. 440.

Japanese people. Indeed, Japan's wartime experiences compelled the creation of a new page in its own scholarly studies. J. H. Kamstra was no doubt correct when he observed that: "Up to 1945, Japanese historians lacked the freedom and the right to [study the origin of the Japanese state]. Excessive nationalism formed an obstacle for a long time to these studies."[26]

Similar observations can be made with regard to other scholarly investigations of ancient Japan. Two related but qualitatively different perspectives and approaches characterize the post-war scholarship on ancient Japan. The first, which could be characterized as "modern Western Japanology," is a sophisticated approach rooted in traditional Japanology, yet greatly enriched by the contributions both of up-to-date humanistic scholarship and of the social sciences—for example, psychology, sociology, and cultural anthropology—all of which are being interfused to disclose the hitherto unearthed meanings of the historical Japanese tradition. Some scholars who subscribe to this approach also appropriate neo-Marxist insights and post-structuralist criticism, among other perspectives, to enhance their methods.

The second approach might be called "neoclassicism." It is a new spirit or attitude because it is critical of traditional Japanology, arguing that the peculiarly Western concepts, categories, and logic that dominate its perspectives and methods may not be the best tools for our study of ancient Japanese traditions. In other words, what the second approach aims to achieve in the study of the historical Japanese tradition is a "re-visioning" and not simply a "revising" of our methods and data in accordance with more modern (Westernized) scholarship. Donald Philippi's study of *norito* as a "performed text" of ancient Japanese religion is an excellent example of this second approach. (It must be pointed out, however, that this "second approach" remains relatively unknown today among many Japanologists in both Japan and the West.)

ANCIENT JAPANESE RELIGION

I was very impressed by Donald Philippi's work when I first became acquainted with it, in the form of a translation of the little-known ancient inscription called "Songs on the Buddha's Foot-Prints."[27] Evidently, this inscription

---

26) J. H. Kamstra, *Encounter or Syncretism: The Initial Growth of Japanese Buddhism* (Leiden, Holland: E. J. Brill, 1967), p. 22.

27) Donald L. Philippi, "Songs on the Buddha's Foot-Prints," *Nihonbunka-Kenkyūsho-Kiyō* no. 2 (1958): 145–48.

caught Philippi's attention because the text's anonymous Japanese poet used the inherited, native tradition of the divine visitor from beyond the sea (*marebito* or *marōdo*) to frame the event of the Buddha's coming, rather than using the usual Buddhist rationale. Indeed, so much of the ancient Japanese tradition, like mother-of-pearl, has many shades and meanings, which can be interpreted differently when seen from various perspectives. Such elusiveness is the intellectual challenge of the ancient Japanese tradition.

Fascinating though the study of Japan's prehistory may be (and there have been considerable advances made in this field during the post-war period), we will not take it up as part of our agenda here.[28] For in spite of numerous theories and hypotheses proposed by scholars in recent years concerning Japan's early history, it remains the case that their conclusions lack consensus on many key points. For the most part, scholars are stymied by the paucity of convincing materials. The two earliest mytho-historical writings, the *Kojiki* ("The Ancient Matters")—which incidentally was retranslated by Philippi[29]—and the *Nihongi* ("Chronicles of Japan"),[30] were compiled in the eighth century, two or three centuries after Japan had been exposed to Sino-Korean civilization and Buddhism. Even though they, and a series of local topologies called the *Fudoki*,[31] no doubt contain many ancient indigenous materials, it is extremely difficult to decide which legends or historical accounts are free from later foreign influences. Even the *Man'yōshū* (the so-called "Myriad Leaves"),[32] the earliest collection of Japanese verses, betrays infiltration by some Buddhistic themes.

Nevertheless, many scholars have pieced together as evidence the scattered references to Japan in Chinese and Korean documents, in a yeomanly effort to reconstruct various facets of ancient Japanese life, despite the fact

---

28) Those who are interested in this subject are referred to Joseph M. Kitagawa, "Prehistoric Background of Japanese Religion," *History of Religions* 2, no. 2 (Winter 1963): 292–328; reprinted in Kitagawa, *On Understanding Japanese Religion*, pp. 3–40.

29) It is instructive to compare Donald Philippi's new translation of *Kojiki* (Princeton: Princeton University Press, and Tokyo: University of Tokyo Press, 1968) with the old translation by the nineteenth century's leading Japanologist, Basil Hall Chamberlain, trans., "*Ko-ji-ki*: Records of Ancient Matters," *Supplement to TASJ* 10 (1882).

30) William George Aston, trans., *Nihongi: Chronicles of Japan from the Earliest Times to A.D. 697* (two volumes in one now available from Rutland and Tokyo: C. E. Tuttle, 1972).

31) Two of them are available in English now: Michiko Yamaguchi Aoki, trans., *Izumo Fudoki* (Tokyo: Sophia University, 1971); and Morita Tohru, ed., "*Hitachi Fudoki*," *Traditions* 1, no. 2 (1976): 23–47, and 1, no. 3 (1977): 55–78.

32) See the Nippon Gakujutsu Shinkōkai translation of *The Manyōshū* (reissued, New York: Columbia University Press, 1965).

that the reality of ancient Japanese life, on both the individual and the collective levels, clearly defies many of the modern categories derived from the Western division of human experience. Take, for example, the term *uji*, which, though usually translated into English as "lineage group," or "clan," was essentially an all-embracing reality, referring, among other things, to a sociological, economic, political, and religious solidarity unit.[33] Another term that has engendered an endless amount of confusion is *kami*, often translated as "deity," "spirit," or "above," but probably more profitably rendered as "sacred," because the ancient Japanese seem to have accepted the sacrality of the total world as permeated by the *kami* ("sacred") nature; thus, by implication, they also affirmed the plurality of the *kami* as separate beings, though without any moralistic qualifications attached to them.[34]

As far as we can ascertain, the ancient Japanese took it for granted that the world was confined to that known to them in the Japanese islands. They also affirmed that the natural world was the sacred, original world, and that there was no order of meaning behind the world experienced by them—at least until later, when, from Chinese civilization and Buddhism, they learned other ways of perceiving the world. In modern lingo: They lived close to the hallowed world of nature.[35] As for the patriarchal *uji* ("lineage") system, many scholars think it was originally of Altaic origin, and that it became a dominant pattern early in Japan's history.[36] Each *uji* had *uji-bito* ("clansmen and -women") with professional service personnel and slaves. The life of each *uji* centered around the *uji-gami* ("*kami* of the *uji*"), who was usually attended to by the *uji-no-kami* ("*uji*-chieftain"). It is believed that the *uji*-chieftain owned the land and people in his jurisdiction, and it was he who directed all the activities of the *uji*, including its economics and agriculture.

---

33)   For the relationships between *uji* and other terms, see Richard J. Miller, *Ancient Japanese Nobility: The Kabane Ranking System* (Berkeley: University of California Press, 1974).

34)   Tsuda Sōkichi wrote a careful exposition of this subject in his article, "The Idea of *Kami* in Ancient Japanese Classics," *T'oung Pao* 52 (1966): chaps. 4–5.

35)   According to Langdon Warner, "No tree could be marked for felling, no bush tapped for lacquer juice, no oven built for smelting or for pottery, and no forge fire lit without appeal to the *kami* residing in each." Langdon Warner, *The Enduring Art of Japan* (Cambridge: Harvard University Press, 1952), p. 19.

36)   Shortly after the end of World War II, some scholars advanced "invasion theories," speculating that an alien group migrated to Japan during its early history and superimposed its beliefs, cultural fashions, and even the *uji* system on the country. Evidently, the "invasion theory" is not very influential today. See Egami Namio, *The Formation of the People and the Origin of the State in Japan* (Tokyo: Tōyō Bunko, Memoirs of the Research Department, no. 23, 1967); and Gary Ledyard, "Galloping along with the Horseriders: Looking for the Founders of Japan," *Journal of Japanese Studies* 1, no. 2 (1975): 217–54.

If we view Japan's broad historical canvas, we note that sometime during the early centuries of the Common Era there developed the so-called Yamato kingdom, which was in essence a primitive tribal-feudalistic confederation of semi-autonomous *uji*-based social, cultural, religious, and political units; its ruler, or rather the head of its ruling *uji* (later called the "imperial house"), was more like a *primus inter pares* than an absolute monarch. In time, Yamato rulers paid tribute to Chinese courts, from which they received kingly titles. The Yamato leader was basically the chieftain of his *uji*, and it was his binding duty to serve (*matsurau*) his *uji* ancestral spirits; yet he was simultaneously a ruler, and as such, had to attend to the political administration (*matsuri-goto*) of the Yamato federation according to the divine will transmitted to him through dreams and divinations. As Manabu Waida rightly observes, the chieftain of the ruling *uji*, having received his kingly title from China, bestowed the sacred seed for the rice field upon his subjects and conferred various court ranks on them.[37] In other words, the ruler's performance of religious ceremonials (*matsuri*) to serve his *uji* ancestral spirits and his carrying out of the duties of political administration (*matsuri-goto*) were considered to be two sides of the same coin.

The course of historical events in East Asia from the fourth century onward brought Japan close to the Asiatic continent; hence, Japan was destined to fall under the strong influence of both Chinese civilization (notably, Confucianism, Taoism, Legalism, and the Yin-Yang system, as well as Chinese legal, educational, and political traditions) and Buddhism. This development resulted in the need to create appropriate designations for the hitherto unnamed and unsystematized indigenous magico-religious-cultic traditions in Japan, so that they could be integrated into the necessarily changed social and political orders. Accordingly, a Sinicized term, *Shinto*, was adopted to signify the "way of the *kami*" (*Kannagara*). Then, inspired by China's unification by the Sui dynasty in A.D. 581, the Yamato leaders in Japan made every effort to unify the nation, leading them to establish the first, self-conscious, major form of religious/cultural/social/economic/political synthesis, the Ritsuryō ("imperial edict") system. Elsewhere, I have explained that the Ritsuryō synthesis—a form of "immanental theocracy"—anchored itself upon three major principles: 1) mutual dependence between the "sovereign's law"—a blending

---

37) See Manabu Waida, "Sacred Kingship in Early Japan: A Historical Introduction," *History of Religions* 15, no. 4 (May 1976): 319–42.

of the indigenous way of the *kami* underlying the monarchical claim and the continental features taken from Confucianism, Taoism, Legalism, and the Yin-Yang system—and "Buddha's Law" (*ōbō-Buppō*); 2) Shinto-Buddhist institutional syncretism (*Shin-Butsu Shūgō*); and 3) belief in Japanese deities as manifestations of the Buddhas and Bodhisattvas in India (*Honji Suijaku*).[38]

The Ritsuryō paradigm attempted to establish a "soteriological community" in Japan, with the sovereign serving in three capacities simultaneously. First, the sovereign was the ruler of the nation. Second, he was the nation's supreme priest. Third, he was the living or Manifest *kami* (*Akitsu-Kami*), and as such wielded power on two counts: 1) as a genealogical descendant of his *uji* ancestress, Amaterasu-Ō-mikami (whose gender was fixed as female by the sixth or seventh century), and, due to her "divine" commandment, was thus entitled to govern the nation; and 2) as the Manifest *kami*, the sovereign was inherently the object of peoples' veneration and worship. In short, the sacrality of the imperial system was believed to provide "cosmic legitimation" to the Ritsuryō synthesis. Accordingly, the stylized court rituals were propagated as the earthly replica of the heavenly rituals as told in myths.

Although the Ritsuryō polity acknowledged the mutual dependence between the sovereign's and the Buddha's laws, the government's real intention was to place narrow restrictions on the Buddhist religion, as exemplified by the "Law Governing Monks and Nuns,"[39] which tried to keep them within the walls of monasteries and nunneries. Evidently, however, the government could not prevent numerous activities of popular Buddhist movements led by various types of unauthorized clerics.

The most revealing aspect of the Ritsuryō paradigm was the structure of its central government, which was divided into two separate departments of equal standing, namely, the Department of *Kami*- or Shinto-Affairs (*Jingi-kan*), in charge of all sacred ceremonials (*matsuri*), and the Great Council of State (*Dajō-kan*), in charge of political administration (*matsuri-goto*). Such a dual structure symbolized the underlying principle of the unity of religion and state (*saisei-itchi*). (It is interesting to note that the Yin-Yang Bureau, known variously as *On'yō-ryō* or *On'myō-ryō*, which was in charge of the observation of heavenly movements, geomancy, fortune-telling, and exorcism, was estab-

---

38) See the "Introduction" to Kitagawa, *On Understanding Japanese Religion*, pp. xii–xiii.
39) See W-T Chan, I. R. al Fārūqī, J. M. Kitagawa, and P. T. Raju, *The Great Asian Religions: An Anthology* (New York: Macmillan, 1969), pp. 258–59.

lished within the Council of State and not within the Department of *Kami*-Affairs.)[40]

The leaders of the Ritsuryō government were astute enough to recognize the importance of history, and it was they who were responsible for the compilation of the two mytho-historical writings mentioned earlier, the *Kojiki* and the *Nihongi*. They also generated many writings dealing with administration, including the *ritsu* (a sort of penal code) and the *ryō* (administrative and civil codes). In principle, however, the entire body of rules and laws was subservient to the sovereign's *semmyō* ("imperial proclamations"), which, unlike *choku* ("edicts"), were believed to be "revealed words issued by the living *kami*." Even so, the Ritsuryō government was determined to compile a collection of minute administrative regulations, court laws, and rules on etiquette. The actual undertaking of such an ambitious collection, however, did not begin until 905, the fifth year of the Engi Era; hence this collection came to be called the *Engi-shiki* ("Procedures of the Engi Era"). (Although it was completed in 927, it was not promulgated until 967. Ironically, by that time much of the compilation proved to be too cumbersome to be applied in actual situations of governmental administration.) The first ten books of the *Engi-shiki*, which deal with various aspects of Shinto—for example, the festivals of the four seasons, extraordinary festivals, the Grand Shrine of Ise, and the Enthronement of a new sovereign—have been regarded as authoritative guides in Shinto affairs. Fortunately, Felicia Bock has provided us with an excellent English translation of the first ten chapters.[41] Significantly, Book Eight is devoted to twenty-seven *norito* ("ritual prayers"), the oldest segment (according to present scholarship) within the *Engi-shiki*, and the subject of Donald Philippi's study.

NORITO, THE PERFORMED TEXTS OF ANCIENT JAPANESE RITUAL PRAYERS

Etymology and Development of *Norito*

Norito is a compound word. As Felicia Bock explains:

The first part, *nori*, is the conjunctive stem of the verb *noru*—to tell, recite, command (superior to inferior), reveal (as the divine will), de-

---

40) See Felicia G. Bock, trans. and annot., *Classical Learning and Taoist Practices in Early Japan* (Tempe: Arizona State University Center for Asian Studies, Occasional Paper no. 17, 1985).

41) Felicia G. Bock, trans. (with introduction and notes), *Engi-Shiki: Procedures of the Engi Era*, vols. 1 and 2 (Tokyo: Sophia University, 1970 and 1972).

cree—and the second part is *to*, a noun. *To* has been taken by some scholars of the past to stand for *koto*, but that would be redundant in this case. The theory of modern scholars . . . is that *to* means a spell or magical device. Thus the compound *norito* would mean the chanting or reciting of the spell. The combined form of *norito-koto* then is "words for reciting a spell."[42]

Bock also points out that:

> Cognates of *noru* are: *inoru*, to pray; *nori*, law, rule; *norou*, to curse, to imprecate; *noroi*, a curse, a malediction; *noberu* or *noburu*, to tell, express, relate, narrate, state; *notama(f)u*, to speak, to tell (superior to inferior). . . . Cognates of the archaic word *to*, a spell, are: *tona(f)u*, to make sounds, and the verb *tonaeru*, to name or call.[43]

Although the origin of *norito* is shrouded in the misty past, it is safe to conjecture that in earlier days there was no fixed form of *norito* as such. Rather, the phenomenon in question—which later came to be classified as *norito*—most likely embraced a wide variety of prayers, charms, and spells that had been developed in different places by respective *uji*-s.

During the early centuries of the Common Era, with the gradual formation of the Yamato kingdom, the ceremonial traditions of various *uji*-s began to be integrated into that of the ruling *uji*. Through it all, it was the intent of the chieftain of the ruling *uji* to appropriate the worship of the *kami* claimed by other *uji* chieftains as belonging to their *uji*-s.[44] Increasingly, divinities of various *uji*-s became integrated into the pantheon of the ruling *uji* tradition, and the corresponding ritual forms of originally disparate groups, such as prayers and incantations, also became more centralized within the framework of the ruling *uji*.

The increasing importance of Shinto as the spiritual engine of the ruling *uji* advanced the cause and prestige of hereditary priestly families within their ranks. As might be expected, the Taika ("Great Change") Reform, which inaugurated the Ritsuryō synthesis in 645, also affirmed the principle of *saisei-itchi* ("unity of religion and government"). Subsequently, the Urabe family, which had established itself as the leading priestly family of the court, in charge of composing and reciting ritual prayers (*norito*), was given the new

---

42) Ibid., vol. 2, p. 61.   43) Ibid., p. 62 n. 291.
44) Ishida Ichirō, *Kami to Nihon-Bunka* ("Kami and Japanese Culture"), (Tokyo: Perikansha, 1983), p. 22.

family name of Nakatomi (literally *Nakatori-omi*, or "the one who mediates between the *kami* and the sovereign"); and this family came to monopolize the control of the new Department of *Kami*-Affairs. Many scholars suspect that the Buddhist *sūtra* reading, which came into vogue in Japan after the sixth century, probably influenced the form of *norito* recitation.[45]

Undoubtedly, the task of conforming the Chinese script—with its highly developed pictographs, ideographs, and phonetic compounds—to Japanese words was very complex. Nevertheless, from the sixth century onward the Japanese intelligentsia managed to learn enough written Chinese to write their own historical and official records of the court. One writing system used Chinese characters that were *read* in Japanese; the complexity of such a system, which was used in the *Kojiki*, is such that, as Philippi explains, "the modern reader of the *Kojiki* . . . has a sort of bilingual puzzle which he must decipher as he goes along."[46] Another system disregarded the lexical meaning of Chinese characters and utilized them only for their sound value, with the aim of approximating Japanese sounds. This system was usually referred to as the *Man'yō-gana* (a form of syllabary used in the *Man'yōshū*, or "Myriad Leaves").[47] The method used for codifying *norito* is referred to as "imperial decree writing" (*semmyō-gaki*), and it is on the whole close to the *Man'yō-gana* system. However, in various forms of recorded *norito*, "the stems and undeclined words were [written] in large characters (mostly phonetically used) and the terminations and particles in small-size characters"[48] to facilitate the correct recitation of *norito*.

We are told that the first collection of *norito* was included in the *Kōnin-shiki* ("Procedures of the Kōnin Era," A.D. 810–24); then it was included in the *Jōgan-shiki* ("Procedures of the Jōgan Era," A.D. 859–74). By far the most comprehensive corpus is the collection of twenty-seven *norito* included in the *Engi-shiki* ("Procedures of the Engi Era," A.D. 901–22). These dates are somewhat misleading, however, because some of the *norito*, even when compiled for the first time, were already considered ancient. It is pertinent to add in this connection that Philippi's volume has, in addition to the twenty-seven *norito* of the *Engi-shiki*, five additional texts—two from the *Nihongi*,

---

45) See Tamura Enchō, *Fujiwara Kamatari* (Tokyo: Hanawa-shobo, 1966), p. 20.
46) Philippi, *Kojiki*, p. 28.
47) G. B. Sansom, *Japan: A Short Cultural History* (New York: Appleton-Century-Crofts, 1943), p. 138.
48) Bock, *Engi-Shiki*, vol. 2, p. 59.

one from the *Kojiki*, one from the *Hitachi Fudoki*, and one from the twelfth-century diary of a Fujiwara nobleman.[49] It is safe to assume that the codification of some of the *norito* texts was done in the heyday of the continental influence (i.e., the influence of Chinese civilization and Buddhism) on Japan.

Inevitably, the Chinese literary style left its mark on the way *norito* was composed, for example, its verse prose and its frequent dependence upon "alternating parallelism" (*kakku tsui*). As Konishi Jin'ichi cogently observed, even though alternating parallelism had existed in Yamato songs from the Archaic Age, the appearance of the particular alternating couplets in *norito* was greatly inspired by the Chinese literary model, with which the compilers would have been familiar.[50]

Even from the brief historical background I have attempted, it is clear, I hope, that *norito* is a unique form of stylized prayer that developed out of the tradition of the ruling *uji* in the Yamato kingdom at a time when it was greatly influenced by Chinese civilization and Buddhism. These fixed prayers were recited on various sacred occasions, both at regularly recurring festivals and at special or temporary events, either as words of *kami* uttered to assembled people or as a petition to *kami* on behalf of people. *Norito* also reflects the self-authenticating circular orientation of the ruling *uji*, in the sense that the sovereign, by virtue of his (or her) allegedly being the physical descendant of the ancestress-*kami*, Amaterasu-Ō-mikami, is the legitimate ruler of the nation as well as being the Manifest *kami*. Thus, *norito* has a heavy dose of *yogoto*, a formula for blessing the reign of the sovereign to ensure that the ruler's era will be prosperous. However, it is well to remember that *norito* is not a text of doctrine; rather, it is what might be called "performed text." That is to say, *norito* was not a book of doctrines or dogmas from which people learned the meaning of life and the world; its aim was to provide people with proper orientations for the practical performance of rituals, prayers, and charms.

Hermeneutical Distance

Although from the tenth century onward most Shinto practitioners and courtiers were intimately familiar with *norito*, as well as with such formulas of blessing as *yogoto* and *iwaigoto* (both of which are often classified under the broader category of *norito*), systematic scholarly studies of ancient ritual

---

49) Philippi, *Norito* (1959), p. 1.
50) See Konishi Jin'ichi et al., *A History of Japanese Literature*, vol. 1: *The Archaic and Ancient Ages* (Princeton: Princeton University Press, 1984), p. 306.

prayers as such did not emerge in Japan until the eighteenth century. Oddly enough, it was the philological-philosophical exploration of Chinese classics by a learned Japanese Confucianist, Ogyū Sorai (1666–1728), that inspired a lay Shinto priest, Kada Azumamaro (1669–1736), to apply the former's scholarly method to the study of ancient Japanese language and literature. Soon the National Learning School (*koku-gaku*), to which Kada contributed mightily, grew into an important movement and joined forces with the many disgruntled Shinto leaders and nationalistic Japanese Confucianists who were preparing the way for the royalist cause.

Inspired by the insights of Kada, his disciple Kamo Mabuchi (1697–1769) pursued the study of the literary and poetical works of the eighth century (Nara period), especially the earliest collection of verses, *Man'yōshū* and *norito*. Important though Kamo's study was, it was colored too much by his personal and scholarly agenda.[51] Kamo was firmly convinced that all poetical works after the *Man'yōshū* showed evidence of the ancient Japanese spirit of spontaneity having been corrupted by alien (i.e., Chinese) influence. Another scholar of the National Learning School, Motoori Norinaga (1730–1801), well-known for his massive study of the *Kojiki*, evidently was also interested in *norito*. However, his detailed study of it seems to have been confined only to the Great Purification Ritual (*Ōharaye no kotoba*). Parenthetically, like Kamo, Motoori's study of *norito* depended heavily on his own intuition and conjectures.

Significantly, soon after the exposure of modern Japan to Western nations, some talented Western Japanologists lost no time in pursuing the study of *norito*, as exemplified by Sir Ernest Satow's and Karl Florenz's detailed studies of the subject.[52] In his 1879 article, Satow enumerates various forms of Shinto,[53] and suggests that *norito* is a precious resource for reconstructing the religious tradition of the primitive Japanese.[54]

---

51) See Muraoka Tsunetsugu, *Studies in Shinto Thought*, trans. D. M. Brown and J. T. Araki (Tokyo: Ministry of Education, 1964), p. 113.

52) E. M. Satow, "Ancient Japanese Rituals," *Transactions of the Asiatic Society of Japan (TASJ)* 7, pt. 1 (1879): 97–132; idem, "Ancient Japanese Rituals, Part III," *TASJ* 9 (1881): 182–211; and Karl Florenz, "Ancient Japanese Rituals, Part IV," *TASJ* 27, pt. 1 (1899): 1–112.

53) See Satow, "Ancient Japanese Rituals" (1879), pp. 98–99.

54) Many Western Japanologists of the late nineteenth and early twentieth centuries, influenced by revolutionary views about "religion," were greatly concerned with the origins of the Japanese people, Japanese language, and Japanese religion. See, for example, E. M. Satow, "The Mythology and Religious Worship of the Ancient Japanese," *The Westminster and Foreign Quarterly Review*, n.s., 54 (1878); William George Aston, "A Comparative Study of the Japanese and

The careful, well-researched studies of *norito* by Western Japanologists had the salutary effect of broadening the intellectual vistas of serious Japanese scholars. In dealing with *norito*, or any other ancient text for that matter, both Western Japanologists and Japanese scholars—in their respective ways, to be sure—have been compelled to contemplate such precarious problems as prejudgment and historical distance, both of which were cogently discussed by Hans-Georg Gadamer.[55]

All of us invariably bring some sort of "prejudgment" to our attempt to understand any alien or ancient text. In many instances our prejudgment is modified or transformed in the process of confronting the text itself. Sometimes, however, especially when we have firmly entrenched preconceived notions—for example, a certain political ideology, evolutionary dogma, or doctrinaire religious belief—our prejudgment becomes a stumbling block to understanding the text in question. In the case of the aforementioned scholar, Kamo Mabuchi, the learned student of the *Man'yōshū* and *norito*, his interests in these texts were not simply historical, philological, or literary. He was convinced, as Muraoka Tsunetsugu astutely observes, that the "Ancient Way" was not "simply a way that prevailed in the past. He thought of it as a *Way that emerged out of the past to be followed in the present.*"[56] Accordingly, he interpreted both *Man'yōshū* and *norito* in this light. Another example is the translation of the *Man'yōshū* (therein spelled *Manyōshū*) by the Nippon Gakujutsu Shinkōkai (the Society for the Promotion of Japanese Science). In the preface, which reflects the cultural nationalism of the text's pre–World War II publication, we read:

> The Manyōman lived in a world peopled by multitudes of gods [*kami*] and spirits, genii and fairies. And it is noteworthy that despite the wide acceptance of Confucianism and Buddhism, almost all the gods he sang, or who fed the well-spring of his lyric inspiration, were purely Japanese. They were gods of the indigenous cult which was named Shinto.[57]

Korean Languages," *Journal of the Royal Asiatic Society of Great Britain and Ireland* 3, pt. 11 (1879); Aston, *Shinto: The Way of the Gods* (London, 1905); Chamberlain, "*Ko-ji-ki*"; and Chamberlain, "The Language, Mythology and Geographical Nomenclature of Japan Viewed in the Light of Aino Studies," *Memoirs of the Literature College* no. 1 (Tokyo: Imperial University, 1887).

55) See Hans-Georg Gadamer, *Truth and Method (Wahrheit und Methode)*, trans. Garret Barden and W. G. Doerpel (New York: Seabury Press, 1975).

56) Muraoka, *Studies in Shinto Thought*, p. 126. My italics.

57) Nippon Gakujutsu Shinkōkai, *The Manyōshū*, p. xxxviii.

Such a statement clearly indicates the idealized and narcissistic prejudgment of the pre-war "Special Manyōshū Committee" of the Gakujutsu Shinkōkai, which was proud to claim the lyrical character of the Man'yō verses as ancient Japan's indigenous product. Many Western Japanologists of the past, wedded to their own evolutionary scheme of humankind, were inclined to regard *norito* simply as an example of primitive religious mentality. In contrast, some contemporary Japanese scholars unduly stress the uniqueness of *norito* as enduring, native Japanese religious notions and practices, unsullied by Chinese or Buddhist influences.

Related to the precarious nature of our "prejudgment" is our dangerous proclivity for overlooking the reality of the "historical distance" that exists, as Gadamer often reminds us, between us as modern individuals and the ancient text of, say, *norito*. Also, we seem to separate the "text" from the people who produced and used it. To make the matter more complex, most of us, including Western scholars and Western-inspired Japanese scholars, have been conditioned by Western logics and the provincial Western convention of dividing human experience into the previously mentioned series of semi-autonomous compartments—religion, culture, aesthetics, ethics, economics, politics, and so on. And, when we encounter such ancient texts as the *Man'yōshū* and *norito*, we tend to forget, in our attempt to explain the Japanese world view by means of our own contemporary concepts, syntaxes, taxonomy, or logics, that the ancient Japanese had their own (at least very different from contemporary Western) way of perceiving human experience.

Happily today there is a small (but gradually increasing) number of scholars who are painfully conscious of the problem of "hermeneutical distance"—the combination of deeply rooted prejudgment and historical distance—when dealing with ancient, and often foreign, texts. Donald Philippi's work in the present volume, *Norito*, is a good example of such a perceptive approach to an ancient text. Many readers may have already come across his translation of the *Kojiki*. Fortunately for us, his helpful Introduction to *Kojiki* includes discussions of "The Archaic Japanese Language," "Writing Systems in Early Japan," and "Manuscripts and Historical Criticism"—all of which directly enhance our understanding of *Norito* as well. Especially noteworthy is his serious attempt to reconstruct the ancient Japanese language, its characteristic vowels, consonants, and syllables.[58] And he demonstrates sim-

---

58) Philippi, *Kojiki*, pp. 20–25.

ilar sensitivity to hermeneutical distance in his study of the epic tradition of the Ainu, as well.[59]

Lex orandi, lex credendi, "As We Pray, So We Believe"

Earlier I suggested that *norito* developed out of the tradition of the ruling *uji* in the ancient Yamato kingdom, which soon came under the massive influence of Chinese civilization and Buddhism. This particular combination of internal and external factors enabled the Yamato kingdom to solidify itself and to develop the impressive Ritsuryō system. This system, as already described above, was an intricate interfusing of 1) the earlier confederation of Shinto-inspired tribal *uji* and 2) Confucian, Taoist, Yin-Yang, and Buddhist features. Understandably, the appropriation of the Chinese writing system as the basis of the Japanese written language; the borrowing of Chinese models of educational, legal, and government institutions; and the importation of Chinese and Buddhist religious, metaphysical, and artistic notions brought about great changes in Japan.

Soon—in A.D. 673, to be exact, when Temmu successfully usurped the throne from the reigning sovereign—the Ritsuryō framework was destined to undergo internal transformations. Not beholden to powerful *uji* leaders, who initially were bulwarks of the Ritsuryō polity, Temmu appointed to important court positions only those he trusted, for example, members of his immediate family, scions of the Fujiwara (formerly known as the Nakatomi) house, and other loyal cronies.[60]

It was Temmu who ordered the compilation of the aforementioned mytho-historical writings, the *Kojiki* and the *Nihongi*, no doubt in an effort to authenticate his claim to the throne through the assertion of his alleged genealogical connections to earlier sovereigns and even to solar deities. In addition, he ordered chroniclers to "eliminate falsehoods" from available records, "discarding the mistaken and establishing the true."[61] Following Temmu's command, his court chroniclers "read history backward" in compiling the *Kojiki*

---

59) Donald L. Philippi, *Songs of Gods, Songs of Humans—The Epic Tradition of the Ainu* (Princeton: Princeton University Press, and Tokyo: University of Tokyo Press, 1979).

60) See Miller, *Ancient Japanese Nobility*.

61) Philippi, *Kojiki*, p. 41. Ebersole is of the opinion that "the *Kojiki*, the *Nihonshoki*, and the *Man'yōshū* are all part of the Court's larger historiographic project." Gary L. Ebersole, *Ritual Poetry and the Politics of Death in Early Japan* (Princeton: Princeton University Press, 1989), p. 10. That may well be the case; however, as I shall discuss presently, I am inclined to think that an additional factor entered into the *Man'yōshū* when it was being edited.

and the *Nihongi*.[62] At the same time, Temmu firmly advocated that Buddhism should be established as the religion for protecting the throne and the nation. He was extremely conscious of his own virtue and accomplishment, and as a follower of the Yin-Yang School as well, he aspired to hold "the mean between the Two Essences [*yin* and *yang*], and [to regulate] the order of Five Elements."[63] Evidently, he even used the Taoist term *mahito* ("one who has attained the Taoist Truth") in his own name, Ame no Nunahara no Mahito, while appropriating another term of Taoist origin, *tennō* (designation of a Heavenly Deity), in lieu of the traditional term, *ten-ō* ("heavenly monarch").[64]

Clearly, Temmu must have had a unique vision as the sovereign of the Ritsuryō state, and his descendants wanted to monopolize the throne in his fashion. Thus, according to G. B. Sansom, when Temmu died in 686:

> he was succeeded not by one of his numerous sons, but by his widow, the Empress Jitō. That lady abdicated in 697, and was succeeded by the Emperor Mommu, her grandson, who was then only a minor. . . . The preamble of the edict pronounced by the Emperor Mommu on his succession [reads]:

> "He says: —Harken all ye assembled August Children . . . to the Word which he speaks even as the Word of the *Sovereign that is a Manifest [kami]* ruling over the Great Land of Many Islands."[65]

Under the rule of the successive sovereigns in Temmu's line, all of whom were pious Buddhists and generous benefactors to Buddhist institutions, yet not known for other talents or virtues (despite their claims to divinity), Japan suffered from official corruption, power struggle in the court, financial bankruptcy, and ecclesiastical intrigue. Meanwhile, according to Sansom:

---

62) That is why in a previous essay I used the expression "A Past of Things Present," twisting Augustine's famous expression, "A Present of Things Past." See Joseph M. Kitagawa, "A Past of Things Present," *History of Religions* 20, nos. 1, and 2 (August-November 1980): 27–42.

63) Tsunoda, *Sources of Japanese Tradition*, p. 59.

64) To the envoy of Silla (one of the Korean principalities) Temmu stated, "*Sumera no Mikoto* [Emperor] having newly attained peace [in his domain] under Heaven [*ame no shita*] has now assumed the imperial dignity." My rendering is slightly more literal than Aston's; see Aston, *Nihongi*, vol. 2, p. 324.

65) Sansom, *Japan: A Short Cultural History*, p. 177. My italics.

After Mommu's death, the throne was occupied by his mother, the Empress Gemmyō, who soon abdicated in favour of Genshō, her daughter. She in turn abdicated, in view of the instructions of her predecessors, who had nominated Mommu's son, [Shōmu], then a small child. Shōmu . . . was succeeded in 749 by his daughter, the Empress Kōken. . . . In 758, the Empress Kōken abdicated in favour of the Emperor Jōnin. . . . The ex-Empress Kōken was advised by a monk named Dōkyō who . . . had seduced his imperial mistress. . . . [Soon Jōnin] was deprived of the title emperor . . . and sent to the distant island of Awaji, where he was strangled not long after. Meanwhile the ex-Empress Kōken, having resumed the throne as the Empress Shōtoku, [appointed Dōkyō to a series of high-ranking positions including that of] Hō-ō, a word today used to translate ''Pope,'' and similar to the appellation at that time assumed by abdicated emperors on joining the priesthood.[66]

To make a long story short, Dōkyō's audacious and abortive attempt to ascend to the throne, coming as it did from an unworldly monk, shocked even the lovelorn empress, who had herself taken tonsure just as her father, the ex-Emperor Shōmu, had done before her. Fortunately, the immediate crisis surrounding the throne was averted, so we are told, by the oracle of the *kami* in Kyushu island, who rejected Dōkyō's attempt. In fact, Dōkyō was banished from the capital soon after the death of the Empress Shōtoku.

. . .

Following the death of Shōtoku in A.D. 770, Kōnin, a mature son of the poet-prince Shiki, and not in the Temmu Emperor's line (as were the emperors before him), ascended to the throne. The reign by a well-seasoned and level-headed non-Temmu-oriented monarch gave the intelligentsia of his day a rare opportunity to reappraise Japan's cultural, religious, social, and political self-identity. This subtle and contradictory thrust—affirming much of the reality of the Ritsuryō synthesis, especially the semideification of the sovereign, yet reacting against the dictatorial policies of monarchs in the Temmu Emperor's line while clinging nostalgically to the old Yamato mores, beliefs, and practices as well as to its literature and poetry—characterized the intellectual climate of the late eighth and early ninth centuries. Taking account of these contradictory trends might provide us with important clues as we attempt to

---

66)   Ibid., pp. 179–82.

discern and penetrate the distinct qualities of such works as the *Man'yōshū* (most likely edited during the latter part of the eighth century); the *Kogo-Shūi* ("Gleanings from Ancient Stories," written in A.D. 807); and *Norito* (collected for the first time in the early ninth century).

To be sure, Japanese intellectuals at that time had a realistic understanding and appreciation of Buddhism and of Chinese philosophical, ethical, and legal notions, as well as Chinese literary and poetical styles. (After all, the *Kaifūsō*, or "Fond Recollection of Poetry," the first collection of Chinese verses by Japanese poets, had been compiled earlier, in A.D. 751.) Yet, they were also haunted by a lingering affection for Japan's old heritage that predated the massive impact of Chinese civilization and Buddhism. Curiously, however, they too read history backward in the sense of transposing some of the contemporary traditions familiar to them—for example, the semidivine claim of the sovereigns—to the ancient Yamato heritage.

The prevailing sense of ambivalence that characterized the intellectual climate of the late eighth and early ninth centuries in Japan might be conveniently illustrated by the *Kogo-Shūi*, in effect a lamentation about the once-glorious but by then seriously slighted Imbe family. Although this small volume contains some precious materials about ancient Yamato practices of *kami* worship, its main demerit is its narrow family orientation.[67] In comparison with the *Kogo-Shūi*, the *Man'yōshū* and *Norito*, which share such important notions as the *koto-dama* ("the spiritual power residing in words") and were produced roughly in the same period, are much more pertinent for our purposes.

. . .

As noted earlier, the *Man'yōshū* is a collection of poetic verses that reflects the spiritual and aesthetic ethos of the early Japanese people, with their unusually penetrating insight into words, sounds, and songs.[68] There is good reason to speculate that the ruling *uji* of Yamato was always served by the Ōtomo and the Ōkume, who were, among other things, experts in negotiating with the spirits residing in words (*koto-dama*) and songs. It was they who helped

67) Jinja Honchō, Kokugakuin University, and the Institute for Japanese Culture and Classics, *Basic Terms of Shinto* (Tokyo: Kokugakuin University, 1958), p. 32.

68) See Nakanishi Susumu, *Man'yō no Sekai (The World of the Man'yōshū)* (Tokyo: Chuo Koronsha, 1973), pp. 3–5.

the sovereigns invoke the power and authority of the *koto-dama*; such an act was called *koto-age* (literally, ''lifting up words'').[69] The ruling *uji* of Yamato also kept a number of court poets, who as resident semi-priests offered spontaneous or stereotyped poems on a variety of occasions, for example, the sovereign's official land-viewing (*kunimi*), the enthronement of a new sovereign, or the death of royalty. Many of these poems were later collected in the *Man'yōshū*. The poems in this volume were taken roughly from the period between A.D. 645 (the year of the Taika Reform, which initiated the Ritsuryō synthesis) and A.D. 759, thereby reflecting the checkered development of Japanese civilization, including the penetration of Chinese civilization and Buddhism; the refinement of the poetic tradition (called the *Man'yō-waka*); and the rise and decline of the Ōtomo *uji*, whose members' verses provided the core of the *Man'yōshū* collection. Many scholars believe that the collection was actually edited by Ōtomo Yakamochi around 770, the year of the Shōtoku Empress's death and the ascension of the Kōnin Emperor.

The age of the *Man'yōshū* is usually subdivided into four periods. The female court poets (*o'una*), who were active during the *first period*, were superseded during the *second period* by male court reciters (*kataribe*), including the celebrated Kakinomoto Hitomaro. Incidentally, the ''poems of praise and lament of the sovereign's family'' by Hitomaro had something in common with *norito*'s formula of blessing the sovereign. It was the task of the *kataribe* to craft ''iconic images which 'prove' the divinity of [the sovereign].''[70] The poems of the *third period* included many non-court themes. By the *fourth period* (roughly between 729 and 759), ritual functions traditionally performed in the court by female or male poets were already taken over by new specialists in sacred affairs, for example, Buddhist and Shinto clerics.[71] Given the rapid social and cultural changes that were taking place in Japan during the eighth century, we can sympathize with the determination of Ōtomo Yakamochi (if indeed he was the actual editor) to make references to the meritorious achievements of generations of the Ōtomo *uji* who had served the sov-

---

69) See Ebersole, *Ritual Poetry*, p. 22; and Konishi et al., *A History of Japanese Literature*, p. 100.

70) See Ian Hideo Levy, trans., *The Ten Thousand Leaves: A Translation of Man'yoshu, Japan's Premier Anthology of Classical Poetry: Volume I* (Princeton: Princeton University Press, 1981), pp. 14–15.

71) Nakanishi, *Man'yō no Sekai*, pp. 14–42.

ereign's house faithfully as specialists in words and songs, as poets, as statesmen, and as military leaders.[72]

• • •

Undoubtedly, the intention behind collecting *norito* was akin to that behind the compilation of the *Man'yōshū*: the desire to preserve early Japanese forms of rituals and prayers. Although the collectors of *norito* were fully aware of the enormous power and prestige of both Buddhism and Chinese civilization, they wanted government leaders always to remember the statement made by the Mononobe and the Nakatomi *uji* chieftains in the mid–sixth century, when Buddhist statues were presented from Paekche to the Yamato court: "Those who have ruled the Empire in this our State always made it their care to worship in Spring, Summer, Autumn and Winter the 180 [*kami*] of Heaven and Earth, and the [*kami*] of the Land and of Grain."[73]

As mentioned earlier, there are two distinct types of *norito*: 1) those classified as *senge-tai*, in which *kami*'s words—through intermediaries, of course—are "intoned down" to the people in sentences ending with " . . . *noru*" ("Thus I declare" or "Thus I speak," as translated by Philippi);[74] and 2) those classified as *sōjō-tai*, in which prayers are said on behalf of the people to *kami* in sentences ending with ". . . *mōsu*" ("Thus I humbly speak").[75] Scholarly opinions vary as to which style of *norito*—*senge-tai* or *sōjō-tai*— was more ancient, but it is commonly accepted that many of the older *norito* belong to the first type, as they deal with more "official" or "public" situations. Incidentally, the twenty-seven *norito* texts collected in the *Engi-shiki* are divided into two other categories: those recited on regular, recurring occasions (*shiji-sai*, Nos. 1–22)—for example, the "Grain-Petitioning Festival" (No. 1); the "Monthly Festival of the Sixth Month" (No. 7); the "Blessing of the Great Palace" (No. 8); the "Great Exorcism of the Last Day of the Sixth Month" (No. 10); and the "Festival of the First Fruits Banquet" (No. 14)— and those recited on one-time occasions (*rinji-sai*, Nos. 23–27)—for example, "When the High Priestess Assumes Her Office" (at the Grand Shrine of Ise,

---

72) Ibid., p. 14.
73) Aston, *Nihongi*, vol. 2, p. 67.
74) The following *norito* in Philippi's *Norito*—Nos. I, III, IV, VII, X, XIV, XVIII, XIX, and XXII—belong to the *senge-tai* group.
75) Other *norito*, for example, Nos. II, V, and VI in Philippi's *Norito*, belong to the *sōjō-tai* group.

No. 23); "To Drive Away A Vengeful Deity" (No. 25); and "Presenting Offerings on Dispatching an Envoy to China" (No. 26).

Many scholars agree with Donald Philippi, who observed that "the Japanese scholars love to dwell on the role of the *koto-dama*, the mystical power believed to dwell in words, or in words arranged in certain magical formula."[76] But there is a wide variety of opinions concerning the *koto-dama* itself. I happen to share Konishi's view on the subject. Konishi, citing a *Man'yōshū* poem presented to a Japanese ambassador to the T'ang court—a poem that describes Yamato as "a land where the *kotodama* / Brings us good fortune"—suggests that the *koto-dama* was a "concept formed from an awakening consciousness of the existence of one's own country [as well as the uniqueness of the Yamato language] in contrast to foreign lands."[77] He further states:

> The ideal of the *kotodama* may have been further emphasized by a contemporary perception that the heyday of the *kotodama* was long past. In other words, the *kotodama*, which had functioned vigorously in the Archaic Age, attenuated in the Ancient Age. But as people directed their consciousness toward foreign matters [during the eighth and ninth centuries], the *kotodama* was rediscovered.[78]

Norito also makes reference to many other pertinent beliefs, myths, and practices that enable us to penetrate the spiritual, ethical, and cultic heritage of the old Yamato, for example, *harai* (purification); *kegare* (pollution); *misogi* (a practice in which water was used to remove sin and pollution from the body and soul); *tsumi* (sin); *chinkon* or *tama-shizume* (a cult for the purpose of preventing the soul from leaving the body); and *musubi* (the spirit of birth and becoming).

Though *Norito* is an important resource for our understanding of the religious, ethical, cultic, and devotional life of the early Japanese people, it was not meant to be a book on doctrines and dogmas. It was first and foremost a practical manual for prayers and *matsuri* ("religious ceremonials"), that is, *matsuri* as whole life, *matsuri* as an expression in rites, and *matsuri* as a mental and inward attitude. In addition, Ono Sokyō calls our attention to another

---

76) Philippi, *Norito* (1959), p. 3.
77) Konishi et al., *A History of Japanese Literature*, p. 203.
78) Ibid., p. 204.

aspect of *matsuri*, namely, the importance of the "element of mystery," implying such ideas as "mysterious power," "power of reconciliation," and "power of unity." He emphasizes that the true meaning of *matsuri* "expresses the faith that there is some power which works between the worshippers and the worshipped. . . . It is in this mysterious power that not only *kami* but all human beings are united."[79] That is, *Norito* does not explicate all these beliefs and doctrines theoretically; it simply presents correct forms and prayers for various occasions of *matsuri*. In this sense, *Norito* is in harmony with a well-known Western principle of profound spiritual significance: *Lex orandi, lex credendi*, "As We Pray, So We Believe."

---

79)   Ono Sokyō, "The Concept of *Kami* in Shinto," *Proceedings of the Second International Conference for Shinto Studies: Continuity and Change* (Jito to Henka) (Tokyo: Kokugakuin University, 1968), p. 16.

INTRODUCTION

The extant literature of ancient Japanese ritual prayers is somewhat limited in quantity and scope, being confined to the 27 official rituals found in volume 8 of the Engi-shiki, the compilation of laws and minute legal regulations of 927 AD, and a few other similar formulas recorded in other ancient documents.[1]

The Engi-shiki is a voluminous compilation of minute regulations and customary usages; like previous compilations (also called *shiki*), none of which have come down to us, it was meant to complement and amplify the basic laws contained in the *Ritsu* and *Ryō*, the fundamental laws of the land. The Engi-shiki (meaning the *shiki* of the Engi era) was completed in 927 AD after 20 years of compilation. The *norito* are grouped together in one volume in the same part of the work devoted to the duties and activities of the Jingi-kan (Office of Rites), the government ministry encharged with formal and official worship of the Shinto deities.

The official—one almost has to say bureaucratic—nature of the rituals determines their diction to a great extent. The Engi-shiki rituals are as a rule extremely repetitive. Several of them are almost identical with one another; and stereotyped phrases and sentiments appear again and again throughout with surprising regularity.

The rituals are cast in antique language of the most flowery sort. Sentences are long and loosely-connected; the grammatical relationship of parts is difficult to determine; the meaning of many words is unclear; and everywhere semantic clarity is sacrificed to sonority. Some of the frequent techniques are: repetition, parallelism, long enumerations of names of deities and offerings, metaphors, the use of mythological accounts to explain the origin of certain forms of worship, and the all-pervading sonority.

---

1) In this compilation I have included five additional texts (nos. XXVIII to XXXII), all of great literary quality. Two are from the the Nihon Shoki (720 AD), one from the Kojiki (712 AD), one from the Hitachi Fudoki (after 715 AD), and one from the diary *Taiki* by Fujiwara no Yorinaga in the twelfth century. Thus they all precede the Engi-shiki by 207–215 years, or, in the last case, are 215 years later.

That they are sonorous, in a rather heavy-handed sort of way, is unquestionable. The best of them—the Great Exorcism of the Last Day of the Sixth Month, the Divine Congratulatory Words of the Kuni-no-miyatuko of Idumo, and a few others—often attain a massive, surging power by means of this sonorous language—a power strikingly similar to that attained with many of the same methods by Hitomaro in his Manyō *chōka.*

It is also interesting to note that there is evidence that there was a special musical technique for reciting these rituals, and that there were books of musical notation for this purpose.

However, in most cases, the *Norito* are more interesting to us as examples of ancient Japanese ritual, as a mirror of the religious concepts and the stately ritual language of the ancient Japanese, than as works of great and enduring literary value.

Oddly enough, there is no single universally accepted theory to explain the meaning of the word *Norito.* The element *nori* is plainly related with the verbs *noru* 'to speak,' *inoru* 'to pray,' and *norofu* 'to curse.' The element *to* has been variously explained to mean 'place' (as in *tokoro*), 'word' (as in *koto*), and 'magic.' No matter what the etymology, it is probably safe to agree with one recent writer that in the primitive period, *norito* was "a general term meaning magic by means of words."[1]

Besides the word *norito* (which frequently occurs in compounds such as the one I have translated: "the heavenly ritual, the solemn ritual words" —*ama-tu-norito no futo-norito-goto*), there are other related terms about which there is also much confusion. For example, there are the words *hogahi,* which I have rendered 'blessing,' *ihahi-goto,* which I also understand as meaning something like 'words of blessing,' and *yogoto,* which I translate as 'congratulatory words.'

Japanese scholars have recently been emphasizing the fact that there is no essentail difference between *semmyō* and *norito.* If one were to make a distinction, *semmyō* (usually translated as 'Imperial edict') is the formula used on governmental and official occasions, in addressing the subjects of the throne; while *norito* is the formula used

---

1) Shiraishi, Mitsukuni, writing in Hisamatsu, Senichi, ed., *Nihon bungaku shi : jōdai* (1955), p. 247.

in religious ceremonies, in addressing deities. The *semmyō,* so to speak, "speak down," as a sovereign to a subject, while the *norito,* one would be entitled to expect, use a respectful, subservient form of diction. However, this is not wholly true. There are some *norito* phrased in respectful-style diction; these all end in the formula 'I humbly speak' (*mawosu*). There are also many *norito* in the *semmyō*-style diction, ending with formulas such as: 'Hear me, all of you. Thus I speak' (*kikosi-mese to noru*). The Japanese verbs *mawosu* and *noru* have been here consistently translated as, respectively: 'humbly speak' and 'speak,' in order to preserve, however artificially, this rather important distinction in style.

What are the sentiments expressed in the *Norito*? Some of them, it is true, are petitionary prayers; for instance, the central portion of the Grain-Petitioning Festival *norito* can be summarized: "If you, oh Deities of the Grain, vouchsafe an abundant harvest, such-and-such desirable offerings will be presented to you." However, a close examination of the texts reveals that a large number of the older *norito* contain elements more akin to incantation than prayer. The Japanese scholars love to dwell on the rôle of the *koto-dama,* the mystical power believed to dwell in words, or in words arranged in certain magical formulas. Surely there exist elements of sympathetic magic in, for example, the beautiful passage in the Divine Congratulatory Words of the Kuni-no-miyatuko of Idumo which begins:

> As the white jewels,
> May you abide with hoary hairs

and in the entire first paragraph of the House Blessing Formula of Prince Woke. It is abundantly clear that the ancient Japanese delighted in the pronouncing of "blessings" designed to ensure longevity and prosperity by referring adroitly to, for instance, the abundance of the grass thatched on the roof or the firmness of the ropes tied in place around the beams. It is also quite possible that divine authorship was attributed to these blessing formulas; and that the person pronouncing them, when possessed of the necessary qualifications, assumed the sanctity and blessing-potentiality of the original deity, somewhat like the priest in the Catholic sacrament of the eucharist.

The present translations have been made with the object of rescuing the objective meaning of the texts from the obscurity of their stately style, of incorporating recent exegetical knowledge, and of making them available to the reader in a fairly readable English form. It was felt that voluminous foot-notes would needlessly clutter the pages; information felt to be absolutely necessary for comprehension of the texts has been appended in a glossary at the end, but no attempt was made at a word-for-word commentary. Words and phrases treated in the glossary are indicated whenever they appear by raised numerals.

NOTES ON INDIVIDUAL NORITO

I. GRAIN-PETITIONING FESTIVAL

This, the longest of the *norito,* is a prayer for abundant crops and for the prosperity of the Imperial House addressed to all the deities in the land. It was recited at the Grain-petitioning Festival (Tosi-gohi no maturi) every year on the fourth day of the second month in the capital and in the local seats of government; the officiant was a priest of the Nakatomi (cf. Glossary) clan, who recited it within the hearing of priests assembled from throughout the country. It is believed that the prayer to the Sovereign Deities of the Grain is the essential part, while the other parts are all borrowed from other sources.

II. KASUGA FESTIVAL

This is the *norito* recited at the festival of the Kasuga Shrine in Nara, held twice each year in the second and eleventh months. The Kasuga Shrine was the family shrine of the powerful Fujiwara family, an offshoot of the Nakatomi clan, and its festival was celebrated with great pomp and pageantry. In this *norito,* the officiant, a priest of the Nakatomi clan, prays to the tutelary gods of the Fujiwara family (deities introduced to Kasuga from Kasima, Katori, and Hirawoka, respectively) for blessings upon the Imperial Court and the noble families serving it.

The *norito* is followed by a rubric saying: "The *norito* of Oho-harano, Hirawoka, etc., also follow this," meaning that the *norito* recited at the festivals of the other tutelary shrines of the Fujiwara family were patterned after this.

III. FESTIVAL OF OHO-IMI IN HIROSE

This *norito* was recited by an Imperial messenger dispatched to attend the festival of the Hirose Shrine (in present-day Nara prefecture), held in the fourth and eleventh months. Its object is to pray for abundant crops to the Food-goddess enshrined at Hirose. The *norito* is addressed to the goddess within the hearing of the local priests and those dwelling on the Imperial plantations (cf. Glossary).

Oho-imi (Great Abstaining) is an alternate name for the festival.

IV. FESTIVAL OF THE WIND DEITIES OF TATUTA

This *norito* is one recited by an Imperial messenger sent to officiate at the festival of the Tatuta Shrine (in present-day Nara prefecture), celebrated on the same day in the fourth and seventh months as that of the Hirose Shrine. Its object is to pray for abundant crops and their protection from damage caused by wind and water to the two Wind Deities of Tatuta. The *norito* is addressed to the deities within the hearing of the local priests and inhabitants of the Imperial plantations.

As other *norito,* this *norito* contains a legendary account of the origin of the worship of the particular shrine.

V. HIRANO FESTIVAL

This *norito* was recited by an Imperial messenger at the festival of the Hirano Shrine (in present-day Kyōto) in the fourth and eleventh months in order to pray for blessings on the Imperial Court.

This particular prayer is addressed to the deity of Imaki. In the Hirano Shrine, besides the deity of Imaki, were also enshrined deities called Kudo and Furu-aki, to which the following *norito,* almost identical in wording, was addressed.

VI. KUDO AND FURU-AKI

This was believed to have been recited upon the same occasion as the preceding *norito.* Little is known concerning the nature and origin of these deities, but it is believed that they are the ancestral deities of families of Korean immigrants who married into the Japanese imperial family. Scholars are in disagreement as to the correct reading of Furu-aki.

VII. MONTHLY FESTIVAL OF THE SIXTH MONTH

This was recited at the *tuki-nami,* or 'monthly' festival celebrated twice a year—on the eleventh day of the sixth and twelfth months—to pray for the prosperity of the Emperor and the Imperial House. It was recited by a priest of the Nakatomi clan within the hearing of priests assembled from throughout the country.

This *norito* is practically identical with that recited at the Grain-petitioning Festival.

VIII. BLESSING OF THE GREAT PALACE

This is a blessing or incantation formula to safeguard the palace of the Emperor. It was recited in a hushed voice by a priest of the Imibe (cf. Glossary) clan during the various Palace-blessing ceremonies, which were ordinarily performed on the twelfth day of the sixth and twelfth months (the day after the preceding 'Monthly' Festival of these months) but also on special occasions such as the removal to a new palace, etc.

IX. FESTIVAL OF THE GATES

A blessing or incantation formula to ensure the protection of the deities which guard the gates of the Imperial Palace. It was recited by a priest of the Imibe clan and is believed to have been said directly after the preceding Blessing of the Great Palace. This explains its lack of the usual opening formula.

X. GREAT EXORCISM OF THE LAST DAY OF THE SIXTH MONTH

This is the exorcism formula read at the Great Exorcism (Oho-harahe) held twice a year: on the last days of the sixth and twelfth months. Its purpose was, of course, to remove all sins from the entire kingdom; however, it would seem that sin (*tumi*) referred more precisely to what we would call pollutions. The sins of the nobles, courtiers, and palace functionaries were all rubbed off onto 'sin-bearers'—the 'heavenly narrow pieces of wood' and the 'heavenly sedge reeds' which figure in the ritual—which were taken and thrown into the river.

The *norito* was recited in the presence of a great assembly of courtiers and nobles; it was spoken by either a Nakatomi or an Urabe (cf. Glossary: Diviners); or perhaps each read part. For a discussion of this, see Kaneko, *Engi-shiki Norito Kō*, p. 427-432.

XI.   INCANTATION FORMULA WHEN THE SWORD IS PRE-SENTED BY THE FUMI-NO-IMIKI OF YAMATO

This is an incantation entirely in Chinese spoken before the Emperor by representatives of two Korean immigrant families: the Fumi-no-imiki of Yamato and the Fumibe of Kafuti.

It was pronounced on the day of the Great Exorcism twice a year before the reading of the Great Exorcism *norito,* and the Emperor was presented with two gold-plated swords (the 'golden sword' of the formula) and two human figures decorated with gold and silver (the 'man of happiness' of the formula)—one by each family.

The Emperor breathed upon these in order to transfer misfortune to them.   Thus they became a sort of 'sin-bearer' for the Emperor.

XII.   FIRE-PACIFYING FESTIVAL

This was recited at a festival performed in the sixth and twelfth months—probably on the same day as the Great Exorcism—in order to prevent fires in the Palace.   The festival was celebrated in the four corners of the Palace by the Urabe clan (cf. Glossary: DIVINERS).

The mythological account contained in this *norito* differs in many respects from the Kojiki and Nihon Shoki.

XIII.   MITI-AHE NO MATURI

Literally, 'Festival of the Road-Feasts,' this festival was performed twice a year, in the sixth and twelfth months—on the same day as the Fire-Pacifying Festival—by the same Urabe clan.   The purpose of the ceremony was to offer food on the roads of the four corners of the capital in order to expel any evil spirits who seek to enter from without.

The intention and wording of the formula are quite similar to those of the Festival of the Gates (IX).   It was later performed frequently whenever pestilences or epidemics occurred.

XIV.   FESTIVAL OF THE FIRST FRUITS BANQUET

This rather matter-of-fact *norito* was pronounced at the Oho-nihe no maturi (also Daijōsai, Ōnamesai), the autumn harvest festival cerebrated at the Imperial Court usually in the eleventh month—the date was later fixed as the last day of the Hare of the eleventh month.

In the Engi-shiki, the harvest festival celebrated every year is called Nihi-name no maturi (also Shinjōsai)—New Grain Banquet Festival—while the first harvest festival to be celebrated during the reign of each new Emperor was celebrated with special ceremony and was called by a separate name—Oho-name no maturi, Great Banquet Festival.

On this occasion offerings were sent to all government-supported shrines throughout the country; and the Emperor ceremonially partook of a banquet of the newly harvested grains, which he also presented to the deities. This festival was perhaps the most important of all the yearly religious festivals observed at Court, and documentary evidence shows that it was widely observed among the populace as a yearly harvest festival.

This *norito* was pronounced by the Nakatomi priest before the priests assembled from throughout the country in order to receive the offerings which they had brought. This ceremony was probably only a small part of the rites connected with the festival; this fact accounts for the relative brevity and perfunctory diction of the *norito*.

XV. MI-TAMA-SIDUME NO IHAHI-TO NO MATURI

This *norito* was recited by the Nakatomi priest during the twelfth month when the Emperor's spirit, which had been secured and pacified at the preceding festival called Tamasidume no maturi (or Chinkonsai, Spirit-Pacifying Festival), was enshrined for another year in the shrine Ihahi-to Shinden in the Office of Rites sanctuary.

The same *norito* was recited at similar ceremonies for the Empress and Crown Prince. The *norito,* strangely, does not refer clearly to the purpose of the ceremony.

XVI. GRAND SHRINE OF ISE: GRAIN-PETITIONING IN THE SECOND MONTH; REGULAR FESTIVALS OF THE SIXTH AND TWELFTH MONTHS

This is the first of nine rather business-like *norito* connected with the Grand Shrine of Ise.

This is the *norito* spoken by the Imperial messenger, a Nakatomi priest, when presenting the Imperial offerings in the Inner Shrine (Naikū) at these three high festivals.

XVII. GRAND SHRINE OF ISE: TOYO-UKE-NO-MIYA (SAME FESTIVALS)

This is the *norito* pronounced by the Imperial messenger at the Outer Shrine (Gekū) on the same occasions as the preceding *norito*.

XVIII. GRAND SHRINE OF ISE: DIVINE GARMENTS FESTIVAL OF THE FOURTH MONTH

This *norito* was pronounced by the High Priest (gūji) of the Grand Shrine of Ise during the festivals twice a year—on the fourteenth of the fourth and ninth months—when sacred cloths woven by members of the Hatori and Womi clans were presented at the Inner Shrine and at the Ara-maturi-no-miya (see Glossary).

The ceremony, long in disuse, was revived in recent times and is still performed.

XIX. GRAND SHRINE OF ISE: REGULAR FESTIVAL OF THE SIXTH MONTH

This is the *norito* spoken by the High Priest (gūji) of the Grand Shrine at the regular festivals of the sixth and twelfth months; it follows that (XVI) spoken by the Imperial messenger on these occasions.

XX. GRAND SHRINE OF ISE: FESTIVAL OF THE DIVINE FIRST FRUITS BANQUET OF THE NINTH MONTH

At the Festival of the Divine First Fruits Banquet (Kamu-nihe no maturi—also Kamu-name-maturi) held in the ninth month (at present on October 17), a prince was sent as the Imperial messenger, accompanied by a Nakatomi and an Imibe (later also by an Urabe).

At the festival this *norito* was recited by the Nakatomi.

The festival was one in which the new grains were offered to the deities of the Grand Shrine of Ise.

XXI. GRAND SHRINE OF ISE: SAME FESTIVAL AT TOYO-UKE-NO-MIYA

This is the *norito* spoken by the Nakatomi at the Outer Shrine (Gekū) the day before the preceding *norito*.

XXII. GRAND SHRINE OF ISE: SAME, DIVINE FIRST FRUITS BANQUET

This is the *norito* spoken by the High Priest (gūji) of the Grand Shrine at the Inner and Outer Shrines on the same occasions as the two preceding *norito*.

XXIII. GRAND SHRINE OF ISE: WHEN THE HIGH PRIESTESS ASSUMES HER OFFICE

This is a *norito* spoken by the Nakatomi priest at the Festival of the Divine First Fruits Banquet in which a new High Priestess (cf. Glossary: PRIESTESSES) of Ise officiates for the first time. Thus it follows directly after XX.

XXIV. GRAND SHRINE OF ISE: NORITO ON MOVING THE SHRINE OF THE GREAT DEITY

The Grand Shrine is rebuilt with new materials once every twenty years, and the sacred treasures are moved from the old shrine building.

This is the *norito* used in both the Inner and Outer Shrines when the new shrines are decorated with articles of clothing and furnishings brought from the old buildings.

XXV. TO DRIVE AWAY A VENGEFUL DEITY

This interesting *norito* was recited occasionally at times of pestilence or calamity in order to drive the deities responsible for the misfortune out of the capital and to restore tranquillity.

The *norito* has two sections: first, a section giving a mythological account of the origin of the throne, emphasizing the subjugation of the unruly deities before the Sovereign Grandchild descended from the Heavens; second, a section entreating, almost cajoling, the vengeful deities to go to some other place, and enumerating various offerings.

The ancient Japanese believed that all misfortunes and calamities were the result of the will of various deities, who had to be placated and thus diverted from their harmful intentions. In some cases, as in the Miti-ahe no maturi (XIII), an appeal is made to certain tutelary deities to drive out the ravaging deities. In this case, however, prayer and offerings are presented directly to the wrong-doing deities. The intention is not to subjugate them, but rather to persuade them to go peacefully somewhere else.

XXVI. PRESENTING OFFERINGS ON DISPATCHING AN ENVOY TO CHINA

This *norito,* despite its title, was probably the formula spoken by a government messenger at the festival dedicating a new port at Sumi-no-ye (modern Ōsaka), from which envoys to China set out on their perilous voyages. The contents of the *norito* do not seem at all appropriate for a prayer on dispatching an envoy.

XXVII. DIVINE CONGRATULATORY WORDS OF THE KUNI-NO-MIYATUKO OF IDUMO

This, the last and best of the Engi-shiki *norito,* was recited in the Court whenever a new kuni-no-miyatuko (see Glossary) of Idumo (modern Izumo, Shimane prefecture) was appointed.

The new kuni-no-miyatuko first was appointed in a ceremony in the Dajōkan, then was invested with ceremonial gifts called *ohi-sati-no-mono* in the Jingi-kan (Office of Rites); after these appointment ceremonies, he returned to Idumo and observed ritual abstinence (*kessai*) for one year.

After one year, he returned to the Court and presented offerings (including jewels, a sword, a mirror, rustic cloth, a white horse, two white swans, and many carriages of game—many of these are alluded to in the formula). At this time he recited this formula.

Then once more he returned and observed ritual abstinence for another year, after which period he came once more to the Court and presented the same offerings and recited the same formula again.

This is one of the oldest of the ritual formulas in the Engi-shiki and is praised by most authorities as the most beautiful and impressive of them all.

XXVIII. CONGRATULATORY WORDS OF THE NAKATOMI

This is a formula pronounced by the Nakatomi head-priest in the eleventh month of the year 1142 at the Daijōsai (Oho-nihe no maturi,

Great Banquet Festival, see XIV) held at the accession ceremonies of Emperor Konoe.

Many old books mention that on the accession of a new Emperor to the throne, the Nakatomi recites the 'Congratulatory Words of the Heavenly Deities' *ama-tu-kami no yogoto,* and the Imibe presents the mirror and sword, the sacred regalia. It also seems that this formula was read every year at the Harvest Festival in the Court (Nihi-name no maturi).

The text of the formula appears in the appendix to a diary (called *Taiki*) kept in the late Heian period by the *sadaijin* Fujiwara no Yori-naga (1120-1156). Although the recorded text is of the particular formula read in the year 1142, much later in time than the Engi-shiki, it is believed that it preserves faithfully the old forms, so that this formula is considered as being on a par with those of the Engi-shiki.

After a brief introductory passage, the formula gives a mythological account of divine instructions about the obtaining of sacred water for the Emperor's meals. The second part describes the method in which the ceremonial first fruits have been obtained and presented, and invokes divine blessings upon the Emperor.

XXIX. HOUSE-BLESSING FORMULA (Muro-hogi) OF PRINCE WOKE

This formula, recorded in the Nihon Shoki (720 AD), is believed to be an authentic house-blessing formula of great antiquity; it is certainly among the oldest extant ritual formulas—the Nihon Shoki preceded the Engi-shiki by some 207 years.

According to the Nihon Shoki account, Princes Oke (Emperor Ninken) and Woke (Emperor Kensō), the grandsons of Emperor Richū, fled and went into hiding when their father, Iti-no-be no Osi-ha no miko, was killed by Emperor Yūryaku. The two princes fled to the land of Harima, concealed their names and rank, and were employed incognito as servants of a local ruler called Sizimi no Miyake no obito. In 481 AD, the second year of the reign of Emperor Seinei, their employer held a dedication celebration for a new house (*nihi-muro-hogi*) in the presence of the governor of the land of Harima, Iyo no Kume-be no Wodate. During the night-long festivities, the two princes were commanded to dance. After Prince Oke had first danced, Prince Woke arose and first pronounced this house-blessing formula (*muro-hogi*). Then he revealed his and his brother's identity, causing much astonishment to the assembled crowd.

The first section is a magical formula imparting blessings on the lord of the house by analogy with various portions of the house. The second section contains an invitation to drink, and the third section seems to have something to do with a deer-dance, a common performance in ancient Japan.

XXX.   WORDS SPOKEN BY KUSI-YA-TAMA-NO-KAMI

This formula, recorded in the Kojiki (712 AD), appears to be a fragment of an old *norito* used at the Great Shrine of Idumo at Kiduki. There is an obvious connection with the old practice at this shrine of kindling sacred fire.

According to the Kojiki account, after the god Oho-kuni-nusi had relinquished the rule of his lands to the descendants of the Heavenly Deities, he built his shrine on the beach of Tagisi in Idumo and dwelt there pacified.

The words of the Kojiki continue:

"The grandson of the deity of the sea-straits, Kusi-ya-tama-no-kami, became the food-server; and when he presented the heavenly viands, he pronounced the blessing.

"Kusi-ya-tama-no-kami turned into a cormorant and, diving to the bottom of the sea, carried out in his mouth clay from the bottom; with this he made heavenly myriad flat vessels. Cutting the stems of sea-weed, he made a fire-drilling mortar; with stems of *komo* sea-weed, he made a fire-drilling pestle; and with these he drilled the fire, saying:"

Then follows the formula.

XXXI.   BLESSING FORMULA OF MI-OYA-NO-KAMI-NO-MI-KOTO

This is a formula recorded completely in 4-syllable Chinese verse in the Hitachi Fudoki (a geographical account of the land of Hitachi—in present Ibaraki prefecture—completed probably shortly after 715 AD) as a song sung by Mi-oya-no-kami (Ancestral Deity) about Mount

Tsukuba.

The account behind it is that when Mi-oya-no-kami was visiting the various deities he was refused lodging by the deity of Mt. Fuji, who gave as an excuse that his house was observing ritual abstinence (*mono-imi*) in preparation for the harvest festival (*nihi-name*)—there being an ancient custom of refusing to admit strangers during periods of *mono-imi*. Mi-oya-no-kami pronounced a curse on Mt. Fuji and went on to Mt. Tsukuba, the deity of which, despite the ritual taboo, entertained him warmly. Hereupon, Mi-oya-no-kami, overjoyed, sang this song. That is why to this day, says the Fudoki, no one climbs the continually snow-capped Mt. Fuji, but the people all come to Mt. Tsukuba to sing and dance, to eat and drink.

The Chinese text is easier to translate into English than to reconstruct into ancient Japanese. Because the Chinese text observes a proper rhyming scheme, it may not be a direct translation of a Japanese original, but at any rate it deserves to be included here as an extremely ancient example of a ritual formula.

XXXII. WORDS SPOKEN BY ITODE

This is a formula recorded in the Nihon Shoki (720 AD) as having been spoken in the year 199 AD by a local ruler in Northern Kyūshū named Itode before Emperor Chūai.

When the Emperor made a progress in the vicinity, Itode heard of his arrival and, to greet him, uprooted many-branched *sakaki* trees, which he set up in the bow and stern of his boat. On the upper branches of these trees he hung curved beads of large dimensions; on the middle branches he hung clear mirrors of white copper; and on the lower branches he hung a sword ten hands long. Then, coming to greet the Emperor at the island of Hike-sima in Anato, he presented these as offerings to him and said this formula.

Here again the formula skillfully weaves the items being presented in as material for pronouncing ritual blessings.

BIBLIOGRAPHY OF MODERN WORKS CONSULTED

次 田　　潤,　　祝 詞 新 講　1927

金 子 武 雄,　　延喜式祝詞講　1951

御 巫 清 勇,　　延喜式祝詞教本　1959

白 石 光 邦,　　祝詞の研究　1941

武 田 祐 吉,　　国文学研究　神祇文学篇　1937

同,　　　　　　神と神を祭る者との文学　改訂版　1943

倉 野 憲 司,　　日本文学史　第三巻　大和時代（下）　1943

久松潜一編,　　日本文学史　上代　1955

'Ancient Japanese Rituals' (The Satow-Florenz translations)
　　Transactions of the Asiatic Society of Japan

I. GRAIN-PETITIONING FESTIVAL

(*Tosi-gohi no maturi*)

Hear me, all of you assembled *kamu-nusi*[26] and *hafuri*[26]. Thus I speak.

> The *kamu-nusi*[26] and *hafuri*[26] together respond: 'ôô.'
> The same below whenever 'Thus I speak' occurs.

I humbly speak before you,
> The Sovereign Deities[28] whose praises are fulfilled[24] as
>> Heavenly Shrines and Earthly Shrines[12]
> By the command of the Sovereign Ancestral Gods and Goddesses[27]
>> Who divinely remain in the High Heavenly Plain[15]:

This year, in the second month,
> Just as grain cultivation is about to begin,
> I present the noble offerings of the Sovereign Grandchild[29]
> And, as the morning sun rises in effulgent glory,
> Fulfill your praises[24]. Thus I speak.

I humbly speak before you,
> The Sovereign Deities of the Grain[8]:

The latter grain to be vouchsafed by you [to the Sovereign
  Grandchild[29]],
> The latter grain to be harvested
>> With foam dripping from the elbows,
> To be pulled hither
>> With mud adhering to both thighs—

If this grain be vouchsafed by you
> In ears many hands long,
> In luxuriant ears;

Then the first fruits will be presented
> In a thousand stalks, eight hundred stalks;

Raising high the soaring necks
> Of the countless wine vessels, filled to the brim;

Both in liquor and in stalks I will fulfill your praises[24].
From that which grows in the vast fields and plains—

The sweet herbs and the bitter herbs—
To that which lives in the blue ocean—
    The wide-finned and the narrow-finned fishes,
    The sea-weeds of the deep and the sea-weeds of the shore—
As well as garments
    Of colored cloth, radiant cloth,
    Plain cloth, and coarse cloth—
In these I will fulfill your praises[24].
Before the Sovereign Deities of the Grain[8]
    I will provide a white horse, a white boar, a white cock,
    And various types of offerings,
And will present the noble offerings of the Sovereign Grandchild[29]
    And fulfill your praises[24]. Thus I speak.

I humbly speak before the Sovereign Deities[28]
    Whose praises are fulfilled[24] by the High Priestess[25]:
I speak your names:
    Kami-musu-bi, Taka-mi-musu-bi, Iku-musu-bi, Taru-musu-bi,
        Tama-tume-musu-bi,
    Oho-miya-no-me, Oho-mi-ke-tu-kami, Koto-siro-nusi,
    And fulfill your praises[24]
Because you bless the reign of the Sovereign Grandchild[29]
    As a long reign, eternal and unmoving,
    And prosper it as an abundant reign.
Therefore as our Sovereign Ancestral Gods and Goddesses[24],
    To you I present the noble offerings of the Sovereign Grandchild[29]
    And fulfill your praises[24]. Thus I speak.

I humbly speak before the Sovereign Deities[28]
    Whose praises are fulfilled by the priestesses of Wigasuri[25]:
I speak your names:
    Iku-wi, Saku-wi, Tu-naga-wi,
    Asuha, Hahiki,
    And fulfill your praises[24]
Because in the bed-rock below, where you hold sway, the palace
    posts are firmly planted,

And the cross-beams of the roof soar high towards the
    High Heavenly Plain[15],
And the noble palace of the Sovereign Grandchild[29] is constructed,
Where, as a heavenly shelter, as a sun-shelter[11], he dwells hidden,
    And tranquilly rules the lands of the four quarters as a
        peaceful land.
Therefore I present the noble offerings of the Sovereign Grandchild[29]
    And fulfill your praises[24]. Thus I speak.

I humbly speak before the Sovereign Deities[28]
    Whose praises are fulfilled by the priestesses of the Gates[25]:
I speak your names:
    Kusi-iha-mato-no-mikoto,
    Toyo-iha-mato-no-mikoto,
    And fulfill your praises[24]
Because you dwell massively imbedded like sacred massed rocks
    In the gates of the four quarters;
You open the gates in the morning
    And close the gates in the evening;
If an unfriendly spirit goes from below, you guard below,
    If it goes from above, you guard above,
    And guard in the guarding by night and the guarding by day.
Therefore I present the noble offerings of the Sovereign Grandchild[29]
    And fulfill your praises[24]. Thus I speak.

I humbly speak before the Sovereign Deities[28]
    Whose praises are fulfilled by the priestesses of Iku-sima[25]:
I speak your names:
    Iku-kuni,
    Taru-kuni,
    And fulfill your praises[24]
Because in each of the myriad islands[18]
    In which you hold away,
    As far as the toad can crawl,
    And as far as the briny bubbles can reach—
The narrow land is made wide,

The steep land is made level,
And without omitting one of the myriad islands[18],
You entrust them all [to the Sovereign Grandchild[29]].
Therefore I present the noble offerings of the Sovereign Grandchild[29]
And fulfill your praises[24].   Thus I speak.

I humbly speak with special words in the solemn presence
Of the deity Ama-terasu-oho-mi-kami[1],
Who dwells at Ise:
The lands of the four quarters, upon which you gaze out,
As far as the heavens stand as partitions,
As far as the land extends in the distance,
As far as the bluish clouds trail across the sky,
As far as the white clouds hang down on the horizon:
On the blue ocean
As far as the prows of the ships can reach,
Without stopping to dry their oars,
On the great ocean the ships teem continuously;
On the roads by land
As far as the horses' hooves can penetrate,
The ropes of the [tribute] packages tightly tied,
Treading over the rocks and roots of trees,
They move over the long roads without pause, continuously;
The narrow land is made wide,
The steep land is made level;
And you entrust the distant lands [to the Sovereign Granchild[29]]
As if casting myriad ropes about them and drawing them hither.
[If you vouchsafe to do all this], then in your solemn presence
The first fruits of the tribute will be piled up
Like a long mountain range,
And of the rest [the Sovereign Granchild[29]] will partake tranquilly.
Also because you bless the reign of the Sovereign Grandchild[29]
As a long reign, eternal and unmoving,
And prosper it as an abundant reign,
As my Sovereign Ancestral Gods and Goddesses[27],*

* Or, by the command of my Sovereign Ancestral Gods and Goddesses

Like a cormorant bending my neck low,
I present to you the noble offerings of the Sovereign Grandchild[29]
And fulfill your praises[24]. Thus I speak.

I humbly speak before the Sovereign Deities[28]
    Who dwell in the Imperial Plantations[17],
Speaking your names:
    Taketi, Kaduraki, Tohoti,
    Siki, Yamanobe, Sofu.
Because the sweet herbs and the bitter herbs
    Which grow in these six Imperial Plantations[17]
    Are brought forth and presented
    As the eternal food, the everlasting food of the Sovereign
        Grandchild[29],
Therefore I present the noble offerings of the Sovereign Grandchild[29]
And fulfill your praises[24]. Thus I speak.

I humbly speak before the Sovereign Deities[28]
    Who dwell at the Mountain Entrances[21],
Speaking your names:
    Asuka, Ihare, Osaka,
    Hatuse, Unebi, Miminasi.
Because the big trees and the small trees
    Growing on the far mountains and the near mountains
    Are cut off at the tops and bottoms and brought hither,
    And used to construct the noble palace of the Sovereign
        Grandchild[29],
    Where, as a heavenly shelter, as a sun-shelter[11], he dwells hidden,
    And tranquilly rules the lands of the four quarters as
        a peaceful land,
Therefore I present the noble offerings of the Sovereign Grandchild[29]
And fulfill your praises[24]. Thus I speak.

I humbly speak before the Sovereign Deities[28]
    Who dwell in the Water-partings[33].
I speak your names:

Yosino, Uda,
Tuke, Kaduraki,
And fulfill your praises[24]—
If the latter grain to be vouchsafed by you [to the Sovereign
   Grandchild[29]]
   Be vouchsafed in ears many hands long,
   In luxuriant ears;
Then to you the first fruits in both stalks and liquor [will be presented],
   Raising high the soaring necks
   Of the countless wine vessels, filled to the brim,
   To fulfill your praises;
Of the rest, the Sovereign Grandchild[29] will partake
   With a ruddy countenance
   As the food of his morning meal and evening meal,
   As his eternal food, his everlasting food.
Therefore I present the noble offerings of the Sovereign Granchild[29]
   And fulfill your praises[24]. Hear me, all of you. Thus I speak.

Speaking in special words, [I say]:
Let the *kamu-nusi*[26] and *hafuri*[26] receive the offerings
   Which the Imibe[16],
         Hanging thick sashes over their weak shoulders,
   Have purified and presented;
And let them, without any slightest error,
   Bear them and present them. Thus I speak.

II. KASUGA FESTIVAL
(*Kasuga maturi*)

By command of the Emperor[5],
I humbly speak in the solemn presence
  Of the four Sovereign Deities[28], dread and awesome:
    Take-mika-duti-no-mikoto, who dwells in Kasima,
    Ihahi-nusi-no-mikoto, who dwells in Katori,
    Ame-no-ko-yane-no-mikoto, who dwells in Hirawoka,
    And [his] spouse Hime-gami:

In accordance with your desires, oh great deities,
On Mount Mikasa in Kasuga,
  The shrine posts broadly planted in the bed-rock below,
  The cross-beams of the roof soaring towards the
    High Heavenly Plain[15],
  [A shrine] is established as a heavenly shelter, as a sun-shelter[11];
There the divine treasures are presented:
  Mirrors, swords, bows,
  Spears and horses have been provided;
Garments of colored cloth, radiant cloth,
  Plain cloth, and coarse cloth have been presented;
And the first fruits of the tribute presented by the lands of
  the four quarters have been arranged in rows:
  The fruits of the blue ocean—
    The wide-finned and the narrow-finned fishes,
    The sea-weeds of the deep and the sea-weeds of the shore—
  As well as the fruits of the mountains and plains—
    The sweet herbs and the bitter herbs—
  The wine—raising high the soaring necks
    Of the countless wine vessels, filled to the brim—
  And the various offerings are piled up
    Like a long mountain range.
And I (office, rank, surname, and name) having been designated
  as *kamu-nusi*[26],

Do present the noble solemn offerings,
Which I pray you to receive tranquilly and peacefully
　　As offerings of ease,
　　As offerings of abundance.
[With this prayer] I fulfill your praises[24],
　　Oh Great Sovereign Deities[28].　Thus I humbly speak.

As a result of this worship,
Do, I pray, now and in the future,
　　Bless the court of the Emperor[5] tranquilly and peacefully,
　　Making it an overflowing reign, an abundant reign;
　　Prosper it as eternal and unmoving;
Grant that the many regions, houses, princes and court nobles
　serving therein may be tranquil
　　And that they may serve in the Emperor's[5] court
　　As luxuriant, flourishing trees
　　And may flourish and prosper.
[With this prayer] I fulfill your praises[24].　Thus I humbly speak.

> The *norito* of Ohoharano, Hirawoka, etc.,
> also follow this.

III. FESTIVAL OF OHO-IMI IN HIROSE

(Hirose no Oho-imi no maturi)

I humbly speak the name of the Sovereign Deity[28]
    Whose praises are fulfilled[24] at Kahahi in Hirose:
Humbly speaking her name:
    Waka-uka-no-me-no-mikoto, the patron of [the Emperor's] food,
    I fulfill her praises[24] in her sovereign presence.
And bearing the noble offerings of the Sovereign Grandchild[29],
    The princes and courtiers, as messengers, fulfill her praises[24]—
Hear me, all of you *kamu-nusi*[26] and *hafuri*[26]. Thus I speak.

I present the noble offerings:
    Garments of colored cloth, radiant cloth,
        Plain cloth, and coarse cloth;
    The five types of things[6];
    Shields, spears, horses;
    And wine, raising high the soaring necks
        Of the countless wine vessels, filled to the brim;
    The soft grain and the coarse grain;
    That which lives in the mountains—
        The soft-furred and the coarse-furred animals—
    That which grows in the vast fields and plains—
        The sweet herbs and the bitter herbs—
    As well as that which lives in the blue ocean—
        The wide-finned and the narrow-finned fishes,
        The sea-weeds of the deep and the sea-weeds of the shore—
    All these I place in abundance:
Thus humbly speak before the Sovereign Deity[28]. Thus I speak.

Receive, I pray, in your heart tranquilly and peacefully,
    oh Sovereign Deity[28],
        The noble offerings thus presented
            As offerings of ease,
            As offerings of abundance,

[And of the rest] the Sovereign Grandchild[29] will partake
  With a ruddy countenance
  As his eternal food, his everlasting food.

First of all, in your sacred fields, oh Sovereign Deity[28],
    [As well as the fields of] the princes of the blood, the princes,
      the courtiers, and the common people of the kingdom—
    May the latter grain harvested by them,
    May the latter grain to be harvested
        With foam dripping from the elbows,
        Pulled hither with mud adhering to both thighs—
    May this grain be prospered by you, oh Sovereign Deity[28],
        In ears many hands long—
Then the first fruits in both liquor and stalks
    Will be set up, a thousand ears, eight thousand ears,
    And piled high like a long mountain range,
    And will be presented in the autumn festival.
    Thus humbly speak before the Sovereign Deity[28]. Thus I speak.

Also before you,
    The Sovereign Deities[28] dwelling in the mountain entrances[21]
        of the six Imperial Plantations[17] in the land of Yamato,
    Do I present the noble offerings of the Sovereign Grandchild[29]:
The colored cloth, radiant cloth, plain cloth, and coarse cloth;
The five types of things[6];
As well as the shields and spears.
When I thus present them,
    If the waters which you send surging down
        From the entrances of the mountains[21] where you hold sway
    Are received as sweet [fructifying] waters,
    And if you* prosper the latter grains
        Harvested by the common people of the kingdom,
        Sparing them from bad winds and rough waters,
Then [I will bring] the first fruits in both liquor and stalks,

---

* Singular; evidently refers back to the deity of Hirose.

Raising high the soaring necks
Of the countless wine vessels, filled to the brim,
And will pile them up like a long mountain range.

Thus we, the princes, courtiers, all the many officials,
    The functionaries of the six Imperial Plantations[17] in the land
        of Yamato,
    As well as even the [common] men and women,
Have all come forth on such-and-such a day of such-and-such a
    month of this year,
    And before you, oh Sovereign Deity*, like cormorants bending
        our necks low,
    As the morning sun rises in effulgent glory,
    Do we fulfill your praises[24].
Hear me, all of you *kamu-nusi*[26] and *hafuri*[26]. Thus I speak.

---

* The expressions here are unmistakeably singular and evidently refer back to the
deity of Hirose, rather than the deities of the plantations of Yamato.

IV. FESTIVAL OF THE WIND DEITIES OF TATUTA

(*Tatuta no kaze no kami no maturi*)

I humbly speak before the Sovereign Deities[28]
    Whose praises are fulfilled[24] at Tatuta:
During the reign of the Sovereign Grandchild[29]
    Who ruled the Great Eight-Island Land[9] in Sikisima[30],
Everything from the five grains
    To be consumed with a ruddy countenance
    [By the Emperor] as his eternal food, his everlasting food,
    To the products harvested by the common people of the kingdom,
    Until the last blade of grass,
    Did not come to fruition.
Not only for one year or two years,
    But they were spoiled for many years.
Therefore [the Emperor] commanded the many wise men
    To divine and discover which deity's will this was.
Although the many wise men made their divinations,
    They reported that they could not discover which deity's will
        this was.
Hearing this, the Sovereign Grandchild[29] said:
    'I have thought that the praises of all the deities are being fulfilled
    'As Heavenly Shrines and Earthly Shrines[12],
    'Without forgetting or omitting any;
    'Which deity is it, then,
    'Who spoils and brings not to fruition
    'All of the products harvested by the common people of the
        kingdom?
    'Reveal to me who you are.'
    Thus he prayed.

At this time it was revealed to the Sovereign Grandchild[29] in a dream:
    '[We are the ones who] afflict with bad winds and rough waters
    'All the products harvested by the common people of the kingdom,
    'And spoil them, bringing them not to fruition.

'Our names are Ame-no-mi-hasira-no-mikoto,
'And Kuni-no-mi-hasira-no-mikoto.'
Thus they revealed their names, [and said further]:
'If you present before us offerings
        'Of garments of colored cloth, radiant cloth,
        'Plain cloth, and coarse cloth,
        'The five types of things[6],
        'Providing shields, spears, horses and saddles,
        'And providing various types of offerings;
    'If you establish our shrine
        'In the place where the morning sun shines its rays,
        'The place where the evening sun is radiant,
        'The field of Tatino in Tatuta;
    'And if you worship before us, fulfilling our praises[24]—
    'Then all the products harvested by the common people of
        the kingdom,
        'From the five grains until the last blade of grass,
        'We will prosper and bring to fruition.'
Thus they revealed to him.
Then in the place taught and revealed by the Sovereign Deities[28]
    The shrine posts were established,
And in order to worship before these Sovereign Deities[28] and fulfill
    their praises[24],
        The Sovereign Grandchild[29] causes his noble offerings to be
            borne hither
        And delegates the princes and courtiers as his messengers
        And fulfills their praises[24].
Thus I humbly speak before the Sovereign Deities[28].
Hear me, all of you *kamu-nusi*[26] and *hafuri*[26]. Thus I speak.

I present noble offerings to the male deity:
        Garments of colored cloth, radiant cloth,
        Plain cloth, and coarse cloth;
        The five types of things[6];
        Providing shields, spears, horses, and saddles,
        And presenting various types of offerings.

To the female deity I provide garments;
A golden thread-box, a golden skein-holder, a golden reel;
Colored cloth, radiant cloth, plain cloth, and coarse cloth;
The five types of things[6];
Furnishing horses with saddles,
And presenting various offerings;
Wine, raising high the soaring necks
Of the countless wine vessels, filled to the brim;
The soft grain and the coarse grain;
That which lives in the mountains—
The soft-furred and the coarse-furred animals;
That which grows in the vast fields and plains—
The sweet herbs and the bitter herbs—
As well as that which lives in the blue ocean—
The wide-finned and the narrow-finned fishes,
The sea-weeds of the deep and the sea-weeds of the shore—
These all are piled up like a long mountain range and presented.

If you receive in your hearts tranquilly and peacefully
These noble offerings thus presented
As offerings of ease,
As offerings of abundance,
And if you spare all the products harvested by the common people
of the kingdom
From bad winds and rough waters
And prosper them and bring them to fruition—
Then the first fruits, raising high the soaring necks
Of the countless wine vessels, filled to the brim,
Will be set up, in both liquor and stalks,
Eight hundred ears, a thousand ears,
And will be presented in the autumn festival.

Thus we, the princes, courtiers, all the many officials,
The functionaries of the six Imperial Plantations[17] in the
land of Yamato,
As well as even the [common] men and women,

Have all gathered here in the fourth month of this year

> In the seventh month say: in the seventh
> month of this year

And before you, oh Sovereign Deities[28], like cormorants bending
our necks low,
As the morning sun today rises in effulgent glory,
Do we fulfill your praises[24].
You *kamu-nusi*[26] and *hafuri*[26], receive the noble offerings of the
Sovereign Grandchild[29]
And present them without the slightest negligence.
Hear, all of you, this command which I speak. Thus I speak.

V. HIRANO FESTIVAL
(Hirano no maturi)

By command of the Emperor[5],
I humbly speak in the solemn presence
    Of the Great Sovereign Deity[28]
        Who has been brought hither from Imaki and worshipped:

In accordance with your desires, oh Great Sovereign Deity[28],
In this place,
    The shrine posts have been broadly set up in the bed-rock below,
    The cross-beams of the roof soaring towards the
        High Heavenly Plain[15],
    And [a shrine] established as a heavenly shelter, as a sun-shelter[11].
And I (office, rank, surname, and name) of the Office of Rites,
   having been designated as *kamu-nusi*[26],
    Do present the divine treasures:
        Bows, swords, mirrors, bells,
        Silken awnings, and horses have been lined up in rows;
        Garments of colored cloth, radiant cloth,
        Plain cloth, and coarse cloth have been provided;
    The first fruits of the tribute presented by the lands of the
      four quarters have been lined up:
        The wine, raising high the soaring necks
          Of the countless wine vessels filled to the brim;
        The fruits of the mountain fields—
          The sweet herbs and the bitter herbs—
        As well as the fruits of the blue ocean—
          The wide-finned and the narrow-finned fishes,
          The sea-weeds of the deep and the sea-weeds of
            the shore—
    All these various offerings do I place, raising them high
      like a long mountain range, and present.
Receive, then, tranquilly, I pray, these noble offerings;
Bless the reign of the Emperor[5] as eternal and unmoving,

Prosper it as an abundant reign,
And grant that he may abide for a myriad ages.
[Thus praying] I fulfill your praises[24]. Thus I humbly speak.

Also I humbly speak:
Guard, I pray, the princes of the blood, the princes,
   The courtiers, and the many officials here assembled
   Who serve [the Emperor[5]];
   Guard them in the guarding by night and the guarding by day,
And grant that they may serve in the Emperor's[5] court
   Ever higher, ever wider, always prospering
   Like luxuriant, flourishing trees.
[Thus praying] I fulfill your praises[24]. Thus I humbly speak.

VI. KUDO AND FURU-AKI
(*Kudo Furu-aki*)

By command of the Emperor[5],
I humbly speak in the solemn presence
   Of the Great Sovereign Deities[28]
      Who have been brought and worshipped at the two shrines
      of Kudo and Furu-aki:

In accordance with your desires, oh Great Sovereign Deities[28],
In this place,
   The shrine posts have been broadly set up in the bed-rock below,
   The cross-beams of the roof soaring towards the High
      Heavenly Plain[15],
   And [a shrine] established as a heavenly shelter, as a sun-shelter[11].
And I (office, rank, surname, and name), having been designated
  as *kamu-nusi*[26],
   Do present the divine treasures:
      Bows, swords, mirrors, bells,
      Silken awnings, and horses have been lined up in rows;
      Garments of colored cloth, radiant cloth,
      Plain cloth, and coarse cloth have been provided;
   The first fruits of the tribute presented by the lands of
    the four quarters have been lined up:
      The wine, raising high the soaring necks
         Of the countless wine vessels, filled to the brim;
      The fruits of the mountain fields—
         The sweet herbs and the bitter herbs—
      As well as the fruits of the blue ocean—
         The wide-finned and the narrow-finned fishes,
         The sea-weeds of the deep and the sea-weeds of
            the shore—
   All these various offerings do I place, raising them high
    like a long mountain range, and present.
Receive, then, tranquilly, I pray, these noble offerings;

Bless the reign of the Emperor[5] as eternal and unmoving,
Prosper it as an abundant reign,
And grant that he may abide for a myriad ages.
[Thus praying] I fulfill your praises[24]. Thus I humbly speak.

Also I humbly speak:
Guard, I pray, the princes of the blood, the princes,
The courtiers, and the many officials here assembled
Who serve [the Emperor[5]];
Guard them in the guarding by night and the guarding by day,
And grant that they may serve in the Emperor's[5] court
Ever higher, ever wider, always prospering
Like luxuriant, flourishing trees.
[Thus praying] I fulfill your praises[24]. Thus I humbly speak.

VII. MONTHLY FESTIVAL OF THE SIXTH MONTH

(Minaduki no tuki-nami no maturi)

Hear me, all of you assembled *kamu-nusi*[26] and *hafuri*[26]. Thus I speak.

I humbly speak before you,
> The Sovereign Deities[28] whose praises are fulfilled[24] as
>> Heavenly Shrines and Earthly Shrines[12]
> By the command of the Sovereign Ancestral Gods and Goddesses[27]
>> Who divinely remain in the High Heavenly Plain[15]:

This year, I have provided the regular monthly offerings of
the sixth month:
>> In the twelfth month say: the regular monthly
>> offerings of the twelfth month

> Colored cloth, radiant cloth,
> Plain cloth, and coarse cloth,

And, as the morning sun rises in effulgent glory,
> Present the noble offerings of the Sovereign Grandchild[29]
> And fulfill your praises[24]. Thus I speak.

I humbly speak before the Sovereign Deities[28]
> Whose praises are fulfilled[24] by the High Priestess[25]:

I speak your names:
> Kami-musu-bi, Taka-mi-musubi, Iku-musubi, Taru-musubi,
> Tama-tume-musu-bi,
> Oho-miya-no-me, Mi-ke-tu-kami, Koto-siro-nusi,
> And fulfill your praises[24]

Because you bless the reign of the Sovereign Grandchild[29]
> As a long reign, eternal and unmoving,
> And prosper it as an abundant reign.

Therefore as our Sovereign Ancestral Gods and Goddesses[27],
> To you I present the noble offerings of the Sovereign Grandchild[29]
> And fulfill your praises[24]. Thus I speak.

I humbly speak before the Sovereign Deities[28]
   Whose praises are fulfilled[24] by the priestesses of Wigasuri[25]:
I speak your names:
   Iku-wi, Saku-wi, Tu-naga-wi,
   Asuha, Hahiki,
   And fulfill your praises[24]
Because in the bed-rock below, where you hold sway, the palace
   posts are firmly planted,
      And the cross-beams of the roof soar high toward the
         High Heavenly Plain[15],
      And the noble palace of the Sovereign Grandchild[29] is constructed,
Where, as a heavenly shelter, as a sun-shelter[11], he dwells hidden,
      And tranquilly rules the lands of the four quarters as a
         peaceful land.
Therefore I present the noble offerings of the Sovereign Grandchild[29]
      And fulfill your praises[24]. Thus I speak.

I humbly speak before the Sovereign Deities[28]
   Whose praises are fulfilled[24] by the priestesses of the Gates[25]:
I speak your names:
   Kusi-iha-mato-no-mikoto,
   Toyo-iha-mato-no-mikoto,
   And fulfill your praises[24]
Because you dwell massively imbedded like sacred massed rocks
   In the gates of the four quarters;
You open the gates in the morning
   And close the gates in the evening;
If an unfriendly spirit goes from below, you guard below,
   If it goes from above, you guard above,
   And guard in the guarding by night and the guarding by day.
Therefore I present the noble offerings of the Sovereign Grandchild[29]
      And fulfill your praises[24]. Thus I speak.

I humbly speak before the Sovereign Deities[28]
   Whose praises are fulfilled by the priestesses of Iku-sima[25]:
I speak your names:

Iku-kuni,
Taru-kuni,
And fulfill your praises[24]
Because in each of the myriad islands[18]
In which you hold sway,
As far as the toad can crawl,
And as far as the briny bubbles can reach—
The narrow land is made wide,
The steep land is made level,
And without omitting one of the myriad islands[18],
You entrust them all [to the Sovereign Grandchild[29]].
Therefore I present the noble offerings of the Sovereign Grandchild[29]
And fulfill your praises[24]. Thus I speak.

I humbly speak with special words in the solemn presence
Of the deity Ama-terasu-oho-mi-kami[1],
Who dwells at Ise:
The lands of the four quarters, upon which you gaze out,
As far as the heavens stand as partitions,
As far as the land extends in the distance,
As far as the bluish clouds trail across the sky,
As far as the white clouds hang down on the horizon:
On the blue ocean
As far as the prows of the ships can reach,
Without stopping to dry their oars,
On the great ocean the ships teem continuously;
On the roads by land
As far as the horses' hooves can penetrate,
The ropes of the [tribute] packages tightly tied,
Treading over the rocks and roots of trees,
They move over the long roads without pause, continuously;
The narrow land is made wide,
The steep land is made level;
And you entrust the distant lands [to the Sovereign Grandchild[29]]
As if casting myriad ropes about them and drawing them hither.
[If you vouchsafe to do all this], then in your presence

The first fruits of the tribute will be piled up
Like a long mountain range,
And of the rest [the Sovereign Grandchild[29]] will partake
tranquilly.
Also because you bless the reign of the Sovereign Grandchild[29]
As a long reign, eternal and unmoving,
And prosper it as an abundant reign,
As my Sovereign Ancestral Gods and Goddesses[27],*
Like a cormorant bending my neck low,
I present to you the noble offerings of the Sovereign Grandchild[29]
And fulfill your praises[24] Thus I speak.

I humbly speak before the Sovereign Deities[28]
Who dwell in the Imperial Plantations[17],
Speaking your names:
Taketi, Kaduraki, Tohoti,
Siki, Yamanobe, Sofu.
Because the sweet herbs and the bitter herbs
Which grow in these six Imperial Plantations[17]
Are brought forth and presented
As the eternal food, the everlasting food of the Sovereign
Grandchild[29],
Therefore I present the noble offerings of the Sovereign Grandchild[29]
And fulfill your praises[24]. Thus I speak.

I humbly speak before the Sovereign Deities[28]
Who dwell at the Mountain Entrances[21],
Speaking your names:
Asuka, Ihare, Osaka.
Hatuse, Unebi, Miminasi.
Because the big trees and the small trees
Growing on the far mountains and the near mountains
Are cut off at the tops and bottoms and brought hither,
And used to construct the noble palace of the Sovereign
Grandchild[29],

---

* Or, by the command of my Sovereign Ancestral Gods and Goddesses

Where, as a heavenly shelter, as a sun-shelter[11], he dwells hidden
And tranquilly rules the lands of the four quarters as a
    peaceful land,
Therefore I present the noble offerings of the Sovereign Grandchild[29]
    And fulfill your praises[24]. Thus I speak.

I humbly speak before the Sovereign Deities[28]
    Who dwell in the Water-partings[33]:
I speak your names:
    Yosino, Uda,
    Tuke, Kaduraki,
    And fulfill your praises[24]—
If the latter grain to be vouchsafed by you [to the Sovereign
  Grandchild[29]]
    Be vouchsafed in ears many hands long,
    In luxuriant ears;
Then to you the first fruits in both stalks and liquor [will be presented],
    Raising high the soaring necks
    Of the countless wine vessels, filled to the brim,
    To fulfill your praises[24];
Of the rest, the Sovereign Grandchild[29] will partake
    With a ruddy countenance
    As the food of his morning meal and evening meal,
    As his eternal food, his everlasting food.
Therefore I present the noble offerings of the Sovereign Grandchild[29]
    And fulfill your praises[24]. Hear me, all of you. Thus I speak.

Speaking in special words, [I say]:
Let the *kamu-nusi*[26] and *hafuri*[26] receive the offerings
    Which the Imibe[16],
        Hanging thick sashes over their weak shoulders,
    Have purified and presented;
And let them, without any slightest error,
    Bear them and present them. Thus I speak.

VIII. BLESSING OF THE GREAT PALACE

(*Oho-tono-hogahi*)

The Sovereign Ancestral Gods and Goddesses[27],
    Who divinely remain in the High Heavenly Plain[15],
    Commanded the Sovereign Grandchild[29] to occupy the heavenly
        high seat,
    And presenting unto him the mirror and sword, the heavenly
        signs [of the imperial succession],
    Said in blessing:
'Our sovereign noble child, oh Sovereign Grandchild[29],
    'Occupying this heavenly high seat,
    '[Retain] the heavenly sun-lineage[14] for myriads of thousands
        of long autumns,
    'And rule tranquilly the Great Eight-Island Land of the Plentiful
        Reed Plains and of the Fresh Ears of Grain[10] as a peaceful land.'
Thus entrusting the land to him,
    By means of a heavenly council,
    They silenced to the last leaf
        The rocks and the stumps of the trees,
        Which had been able to speak,
    And [caused him to] descend from the heavens
        To reign over this kingdom
        [As] the Sovereign Grandchild[29] ruling the heavenly
        sun-lineage[14]—
Whose palace is now [built] with trees
    Standing in the large valleys
        And the small valleys of the mountain fastnesses,
    Which are cut down with the consecrated axes of the Imibe[16] clan,
    The tops and bottoms offered to the deities of the mountain,
    And the middle portions are brought out
        And with a consecrated spade are erected as consecrated
        posts,
    And made into the noble palace built for the Sovereign
    Grandchild[29]

As a heavenly shelter, a sun-shelter[11]:
To you, [oh palace deity] Ya-bune-no-mikoto, [do I address]
  marvellous heavenly words of blessing,
    And bless and pacify, humbly speaking:

In the location of the great palace where he holds sway,
    To the farthest extent of the bed-rock beneath,
        May there be no woes from the roots of vines and from
          creeping insects;
    As far as the blue clouds drift in the High Heavenly Plain[15],
        May there be no woes from blood dripping [from the
          heavens] and from flying birds,
    May there be no moving and creaking of the firmly implanted
      posts, beams, rafters, doors, and windows,
    May there be no loosening of the firmly bound cords,
        No disheveling of the grass thatched on the roof,
        No commotion in the flooring,
        No panic and fearful appearances during the night.
I speak the names of the deities who thus tranquilly and
  peacefully give their protection:
    Ya-bune-kuku-no-ti-no-mikoto

        This is the tree-spirit

    And Ya-bune-toyo-uke-hime-no-mikoto

        This is the spirit of the rice plants, commonly
        called Uka-no-mi-tama. This is of the same
        order as the custom of today of placing pieces
        of wood with the tops shaved and bundles of
        rice stalks by the door of a parturition hut,
        and scattering rice grains within the house.

    Thus praising your names—
Because you protect the reign of the Sovereign Grandchild[29] as
  eternal and unmoving,
    And prosper it as an abundant reign, an overflowing reign,
      a long reign;
Therefore, onto the long strings of myriad *mi-fuki* noble beads,
    Which have been purified and sanctified by the sacred bead-makers,

Have been attached colored cloth, radiant cloth;
And I, Imibe-no-sukune[16] So-and-so, hanging a thick sash over my
weak shoulders,
    Bless and pacify—
Grant that any error or omission in this
    May be heard rectified and beheld rectified
        By [the rectifying deities] Kamu-naho-bi-no-mikoto and
          Oho-naho-bi-no-mikoto,
    And that they may hear and receive it tranquilly and peacefully.
    Thus I humbly speak.

I humbly speak with special words regarding the name of
    Oho-miya-no-me-no-mikoto,
        Who dwells massively imbedded within the same palace as
          the Sovereign Grandchild[29];
        Rules the selection of those who go in and those who go out;
        Rectifies by words and soothes the sudden invasions
          and ravages of the deities;
        Prevents from errors of the hand and errors of the feet
          The scarf-wearing women attendants
          And the sash-wearing men attendants
          Who serve at the Sovereign Grandchild's[29] morning meal
           and evening meal;
        Prevents the princes of the blood, the princes, the court nobles,
          and all the officials
          From each following his own separate way;
        Enables them to serve in the palace wholeheartedly,
          To work in the palace energetically,
          Without any evil intentions or impure intentions;
        And if there be any fault or error,
          Beholds it rectified and hears it rectified,
          And causes them to serve tranquilly and peacefully.
Because of this, [I speak] her name as
    Oho-miya-no-me-no-mikoto
    And fulfill her praises[24]. Thus I humbly speak.

IX. FESTIVAL OF THE GATES

(Mi-kado no maturi)

I humbly speak your names:
    Kusi-iha-mato,
    Toyo-iha-mato-no-mikoto,
Because you dwell massively imbedded like sacred massed rocks
    In the inner and outer gates of the four quarters,
Because if from the four quarters and the four corners
    There should come the unfriendly and unruly deity called
        Ame-no-maga-tu-hi,
    You are not bewitched and do not speak consent to his evil words—
    If he goes from above,
        You guard above,
    If he goes from below,
        You guard below,
    And lie in wait to protect
        And to drive away
        And to repulse him with words;
Because you open the gates in the morning
    And close the gates in the evening;
You inquire and know the names
    Of those who go in and those who go out;
And if there be any fault or error,
    In the manner of [the rectifying deities] Kamu-naho-bi
        and Oho-naho-bi
    You behold it rectified and hear it rectified,
And cause [the court attendants] to serve tranquilly and peacefully.

Therefore [I speak] your names:
    Toyo-iha-mato-no-mikoto and
    Kusi-iha-mato-no-mikoto
And fulfill your praises[24]. Thus I humbly speak.

X. GREAT EXORCISM OF THE LAST DAY OF THE SIXTH MONTH

(*Minaduki tugomori no oho-harahe*)

Hear me, all of you assembled princes of the blood, princes,
  court nobles, and all officials.   Thus I speak.

The various sins perpetrated and committed
    By those who serve in the Emperor's[5] court,
        The scarf-wearing women attendants,
        The sash-wearing men attendants,
        The quiver-bearing guard attendants,
        The sword-bearing guard attendants,
    As well as all those who serve in various offices—
These sins are to be exorcised, are to be purified
    In the great exorcism of the last day of the sixth month
        of this year—
Hear me, all of you.   Thus I speak.

By the command of the Sovereign Ancestral Gods and Goddesses[27],
    Who divinely remain in the High Heavenly Plain[15],
The eight myriad deities were convoked in a divine convocation,
    Consulted in a divine consultation,
    And spoke these words of entrusting:
        'Our Sovereign Grandchild[29] is to rule
        'The Land of the Plentiful Reed Plains of the Fresh Ears
            of Grain[10]
        'Tranquilly as a peaceful land.'
Having thus entrusted the land,
    They inquired with a divine inquiry
    Of the unruly deities in the land,
    And expelled them with a divine expulsion;
They silenced to the last leaf
    The rocks and the stumps of the trees,
    Which had been able to speak,

And caused him to descend from the heavens,
    Leaving the heavenly rock-seat,
    And pushing with an awesome pushing
        Through the myriad layers of heavenly clouds—
Thus they entrusted [the land to him].

The lands of the four quarters thus entrusted,
    Great Yamato, the Land of the Sun-Seen-on-High,
    Was pacified and made a peaceful land;
The palace posts were firmly planted in the bed-rock below,
    The cross-beams soaring high towards the High Heavenly Plain[15],
    And the noble palace of the Sovereign Grandchild[29] constructed,
      Where, as a heavenly shelter, as a sun-shelter[11],
        he dwells hidden,
      And rules [the kingdom] tranquilly as a peaceful land.

The various sins perpetrated and committed
    By the heavenly ever-increasing people to come into existence
    In this land which he is to rule tranquilly as a peaceful land:
First, the heavenly sins[13]:
    Breaking down the ridges,
    Covering up the ditches,
    Releasing the irrigation sluices,
    Double planting,
    Setting up stakes,
    Skinning alive, skinning backwards,
    Defecation—
    Many sins [such as these] are distinguished and called the
      heavenly sins[13].
The earthly sins[4]:
    Cutting living flesh, cutting dead flesh,
    White leprosy, skin excrescences,
    The sin of violating one's own mother,
    The sin of violating one's own child,
    The sin of violating a mother and her child,
    The sin of violating a child and her mother,

The sin of transgression with animals,
Woes from creeping insects,
Woes from the deities of on high,
Woes from the birds of on high,
Killing animals, the sin of witchcraft—
Many sins [such as these] shall appear.

When they thus appear,
By the heavenly shrine usage,
    Let the Great Nakatomi[22] cut off the bottom and cut off the top
        Of heavenly narrow pieces of wood,
    And place them in abundance on a thousand tables;
    Let him cut off the bottom and cut off the top
        Of heavenly sedge reeds
    And cut them up into myriad strips;
    And let him pronounce the heavenly ritual, the solemn
    ritual words.
When he thus pronounces them,
    The heavenly deities will push open the heavenly rock door,
    And pushing with an awesome pushing
        Through the myriad layers of heavenly clouds,
    Will hear and receive [these words].
Then the earthly deities will climb up
    To the summits of the high mountains and to the summits of
    the low mountains,
    And pushing aside the mists of the high mountains and the
    mists of the low mountains,
    Will hear and receive [these words].

When they thus hear and receive,
Then, beginning with the court of the Sovereign Grandchild[29],
    In the lands of the four quarters under the heavens,
    Each and every sin will be gone.
As the gusty wind blows apart the myriad layers of heavenly clouds;
    As the morning mist, the evening mist is blown away by the
    morning wind, the evening wind;

As the large ship anchored in the spacious port is untied
    at the prow and untied at the stern
        And pushed out into the great ocean;
As the luxuriant clump of trees on yonder [hill]
        Is cut away at the base with a tempered sickle, a sharp sickle—
As a result of the exorcism and the purification,
    There will be no sins left.
They will be taken into the grea ocean
    By the goddess called Se-ori-tu-hime,
    Who dwells in the rapids of the rapid-running rivers
        Which fall surging perpendicular
        From the summits of the high mountains and the summits
            of the low mountains.
When she thus takes them,
    They will be swallowed with a gulp
        By the goddess called Haya-aki-tu-hime,
            Who dwells in the wild brine, the myriad currents
                of the brine,
                In the myriad meeting-place of the brine of
                    the many briny currents.
When she thus swallows them with a gulp,
    The deity called Ibuki-do-nusi,
        Who dwells in the Ibuki-do*,
    Will blow them away with his breath to the land of Hades,
        the under-world.
When he thus blows them away,
    The deity called Haya-sasura-hime,
        Who dwells in the land of Hades, the under-world,
    Will wander off with them and lose them.
When she thus loses them,
    Beginning with the many officials serving in the Emperor's[5] court,
    In the four quarters under the heavens,
    Beginning from today,
    Each and every sin will be gone.

---

* lit., Breath-blowing-entrance

Holding the horses
    Which stand listening,
        Pricking up their ears towards the High Heavenly Plain[15],
Hear me, all of you:
Know that [all the sins] have been exorcised and purified
    In the great exorcism performed in the waning of the evening sun
    On the last day of the sixth month of this year.   Thus I speak.

Oh diviners[3] of the four lands,
    Carry them out to the great river
    And cast them away.   Thus I speak.

XI. INCANTATION FORMULA WHEN THE SWORD IS PRESENTED BY THE FUMI-NO-IMIKI OF YAMATO

I respectfully pray:
Oh Supreme Ruler of Heaven,
Oh Great Ruler of the Three Extremities,
Oh sun and moon and stars,
Oh gods of the eight quarters,
Oh deities arbiting human destiny,
Oh King of the East on the left,
And Queen of the West on the right,
Oh five rulers of the five directions,
Oh four seasons and four weathers:

I present you with a man of happiness
And pray you to remove all disasters.
I present you with a golden sword
And pray you to extend the imperial reign.

I speak the incantation:

To the East as far as the Land of the Extreme East,
To the West as far as the Land where the sun sets,
To the South as far as the Land of Blazing Light,
To the North as far as the Weak Waters,
May the thousand cities and hundred lands
Be ruled in peace for ten thousand years,
Ten thousand years,
Ten thousand years.

XII. FIRE-PACIFYING FESTIVAL

(*Hi-sidume no maturi*)

I humbly speak by means of the heavenly ritual, the solemn ritual
  words entrusted
    At the time that the kingdom was entrusted
    By the command of the Sovereign Ancestral Gods and Goddesses[27],
        Who divinely remain in the High Heavenly Plain[15],
    To the Sovereign Grandchild[29], saying:
        'Rule tranquilly the Land of the Plentiful Reed Plains
          and of the Fresh Ears of Grain[10] as a peaceful land.'

The two deities Izanagi and Izanami,
    Becoming wedded man and wife,
    Gave birth to each of the myriad lands and each of the myriad
      islands[18],
    And gave birth to the eight myriads of deities;
As their final child [Izanami] gave birth to Ho-musu-bi-no-kami,
    And thereby burning her genitals,
    Concealed herself within the rock and said:
        'For seven nights and seven days do not look upon me,
          my beloved husband.'
Before the expiration of these seven days,
    He thought her concealment strange and looked upon her:
        He found that she was burnt in her genitals from giving
          birth to fire.
At that time, she said:
    'Although I told my beloved husband not to look upon me,
    'He has rashly looked upon me.
    'My beloved husband shall rule the Upper Lands,
    'And I will rule the Lower Lands.'
    Thus saying, she concealed herself in the rock.
Arriving at the pass Yomo-tu-hira-saka, she remembered:
    'I have born and left a child of evil disposition
    'In the Upper Lands to be ruled by my beloved husband.'

Thus saying, she returned and gave birth to further children of
   four kinds:
   The water deity,
   The gourd [dipper],
   The river greens,
   And [the earth deity] Hani-yama-hime,
   And instructed and advised:
      'If this child of evil disposition become wildly disposed,
      'Let the water deity take the gourd, and Hani-yama-hime
         the river greens, and pacify him!'

Because of this, I fulfill your praises[24],
And, in order that he do not wreak havoc in the court of the
   Sovereign Grandchild[29],
   I make offerings:
      Furnishing colored cloth, radiant cloth, plain cloth,
         coarse cloth;
      The five types of things[6];
      As well as that which lives in the blue ocean—
         The wide-finned and the narrow-finned fishes,
         The sea-weeds of the deep and the sea-weeds of the
            shore—
      And wine, raising high the soaring necks
         Of the countless wine vessels, filled to the brim;
      And even to the soft grain and the coarse grain—
   I pile these high like a long mountain range,
And, by means of the heavenly ritual, the solemn ritual words,
   Fulfill your praises[24]. Thus I humbly speak.

XIII. MITI-AHE NO MATURI

[As a tradition which] began in the High Heavenly Plain[15],
I humbly speak before the Sovereign Deities[29]
    Who dwell massively imbedded like sacred massed rocks
        In the myriad great thoroughfares,
    Whose praises are fulfilled[24] by command of the
        Sovereign Grandchild[29]:

I humbly speak your names:
    Ya-timata-hiko,
    Ya-timata-hime,
    Kunato,
And fulfill your praises[24]

[With the prayer] that you will not be bewitched and will not speak
  consent
    To the unfriendly and unruly spirits
    Who come from the land of Hades, the underworld;
If they go below, you will guard below,
    If they go above, you will guard above,
    And will guard in the guarding by night and the guarding by day,
    And will bless.

With this prayer I present offerings,
    Furnishing garments of colored cloth, radiant cloth, plain cloth,
      and coarse cloth;
    And wine, raising high the soaring necks
      Of the countless wine vessels, filled to the brim;
    In both liquor and in stalks;
    That which lives in the mountains and plains—
      The soft-furred and the coarse-furred animals;
    As well as that which lives in the blue ocean—
      The wide-finned and the narrow-finned fishes,
      The sea-weeds of the deep and the sea-weeds of the shore—

These will be placed abundantly like a long mountain range.
Receive, then, tranquilly, I pray, these noble offerings here presented,
 And, dwelling massively imbedded like sacred massed rocks
  In the myriad great thoroughfares,
 Bless the Sovereign Grandchild[29] eternal and unmoving,
 And prosper him as an abundant reign. Thus I humbly speak.

Further, [with the prayer] that you may bless tranquilly
 The princes of the blood, the princes, the courtiers,
  the many officials,
 As well as even the common people of the kingdom,
 I, as priest[26], fulfill your praises[24]
  By the heavenly ritual, the solemn ritual words.
  Thus I humbly speak.

XIV. FESTIVAL OF THE FIRST FRUITS BANQUET

(Oho-nihe no maturi)

Hear me, all of you assembled *kamu-nusi*[26] and *hafuri*[26]. Thus I speak.

I humbly speak before the Sovereign Deities[28]
    Who hold sway as Heavenly Shrines and Earthly Shrines[12]
    By the command of the Sovereign Ancestral Gods and Goddesses[27]
       Who divinely remain in the High Heavenly Plain[15]:

Whereas on the second day of the Hare in the eleventh month
  of this year
    The Sovereign Grandchild[29] is to partake of the banquet of
      the first fruits
    As his heavenly food, his eternal food, his everlasting food,

Because you Sovereign Deities[28], concurring together,
    Deign to bless him as eternal and unmoving
    And to prosper him as an abundant reign,
He will partake tranquilly and peacefully for a thousand autumns,
  for five hundred autumns,
    And will feast with a ruddy countenance at the abundant banquet.

The noble offerings of the Sovereign Grandchild[29] are furnished:
    The colored cloth, radiant cloth, plain cloth, and coarse cloth;
And, as the morning sun rises in effugent glory,
    I fulfill your praises[24].
Hear me, all of you. Thus I speak.

Speaking in special words, [I say]:
    Let the *kamu-nusi*[26] and *hafuri*[26] receive the offerings
      Which the Imibe[16],
         Hanging thick sashes over their weak shoulders,
         Have purified and presented,
  And let them, without the slightest omission,
    Bear them and present them. Thus I speak.

XV. MI-TAMA-SIDUME NO IHAHI-TO
NO MATURI

By the command of the Sovereign Ancestral Gods and Goddesses[27],
    Who divinely remain in the High Heavenly Plain[15],
The Sovereign Grandchild[29], making the Land of the Plentiful Reed
    Plains and of the Fresh Ears of Grain[10] a peaceful land,
        And firmly rooting the shrine posts in the bed-rock below,
            The cross-beams of the roof soaring high towards the
                High Heavenly Plain[15],
        As a heavenly shelter, as a sun-shelter[11],
        Does fulfill your praises[24],
And present garments, providing both the upper and the lower garments,
    And his noble offerings:
            Colored cloth, radiant cloth, plain cloth, and coarse cloth;
            The five types of things[6];
            And wine, raising high the soaring necks
                Of the countless wine vessels, filled to the brim;
            The fruits of the mountains and plains—
                The sweet herbs and the bitter herbs—
            As well as the fruits of the blue ocean—
                The wide-finned and the narrow-finned fishes,
                The sea-weeds of the deep and the sea-weeds of the
                    shore—
    All these various offerings he places and raises high like a
        long mountain range, and presents them.

Receive, then, tranquilly, I pray, these noble offerings
        As offerings of peace,
        As offerings of plenty;
Bless the court of the Emperor[5] as eternal and unmoving,
        Prosper it as an abundant reign,
And grant that [his spirit] may abide tranquilly here in its abode
        From this twelfth month
        Until the twelfth month to come.
With this prayer, on the such-and-such day of the twelfth month of
    this year,
        I bless and pacify [his spirit]. Thus I humbly speak.

XVI. GRAND SHRINE OF ISE: GRAIN-PETITIONING IN THE SECOND MONTH; REGULAR FESTIVALS OF THE SIXTH AND TWELFTH MONTHS

By the solemn command of the Emperor[5],
I humbly speak before you,
    Great Sovereign Deity[28], whose praises are fulfilled[24]
        In the bed-rock below
        On the upper reaches of the Isuzu river
        At Udi in Watarahi:

I humbly speak his solemn command
    To bring and present the great offerings
        Habitually presented at the Grain-petitioning of the
        Second month

> At the regular festivals merely replace with the words:
> at the regular festival of the sixth month

Sending me (office, rank, surname, name) as his messenger.
Thus I humbly speak.

XVII. GRAND SHRINE OF ISE: TOYO-UKE-NO-MIYA
(SAME FESTIVALS)

By the solemn command of the Emperor[5],
I humbly speak before you,
    Toyo-uke-no-sume-gami,
    Whose praises are fulfilled[24]
    In the bed-rock below
    Of the field of Yamada in Watarahi:

I humbly speak his solemn command
    To bring and present the great offerings
        Habitually presented at the Grain-petitioning of the
        second month

        At the regular festivals merely replace with the words:
        at the regular festival of the sixth month

    Sending me (office, rank, surname, name) as his messenger.
    Thus I humbly speak.

XVIII. GRAND SHRINE OF ISE: DIVINE GARMENTS FESTIVAL OF THE FOURTH MONTH
(*Uduki no Kamu-miso no maturi*)

(*Use also for that of the ninth month*)

I humbly speak in the solemn presence
    Of Ama-terasi-masu-sume-oho-mi-kami[1],
        Whose praises are fulfilled[24],
        Where the great shrine posts are firmly planted
            And the cross-beams of the roof soar towards the
                High Heavenly Plain[15],
        In the upper reaches of the Isuzu river
        At Udi in Watarahi:

I humbly say that the presentation is made
    Of the woven garments of plain cloth and coarse cloth
        Habitually presented
            By the people of the Hatori and the Womi.
Thus I humbly speak.

Say this and present them
    Also in the Ara-maturi-no-miya[2]. Thus I speak.

        The *negi*[26] and *uti-bito*[26] together respond: 'ôô.'

XIX. GRAND SHRINE OF ISE: REGULAR FESTIVAL
OF THE SIXTH MONTH

(Use also for that of the Twelfth Month)

All of you *kamu-nusi-be*[26] and *mono-imi*[26], hear the heavenly ritual,
the solemn ritual words
  Which I humbly speak in the solemn presence of
  Ama-terasi-masu-oho-mi-kami[1],
    Whose praises are fulfilled[24],
      With the great shrine-posts firmly rooted
      And the cross-beams of the roof soaring high towards
      the High Heavenly Plain[15],
    On the upper reaches of the Isuzu river
    At Udi in Watarahi. Thus I speak.

      The *negi*[26] and *uti-bito*[26] together respond: 'ôô.'

By the solemn command of the Emperor[5],
[I pray] that you make his life a long life,
  Prospering [his reign] as an abundant reign,
  Eternal and unmoving as the sacred massed rocks,
That you favor also the princes which are born,
That you [protect] long and tranquilly
  The various officials,
  As well as even the common people of the lands of the four
    quarters of the kingdom,
And that you cause to flourish in abundance
  The five grains which they harvest.
With this prayer [I offer]
  The tribute threads habitually presented by the people
  of the Kamube[19]
    Established in the three counties and in the various lands
      and various places,
  And the great wine and the great first fruits prepared in
    ritual purity,

Placing these in abundance like a long mountain range.
I, the great Nakatomi[22], abiding concealed behind
   the solemn *tama-gusi*[31]
On the seventeenth day of the sixth month of this year,
Do humbly speak your praises as the morning sun rises in effugent glory.
Hear me, all of you *kamu-nusi-be*[26] and *mono-imi*[26].   Thus I speak.

   The *kamu-nusi-be*[26] together respond: 'ôô.'

Say this and present them
   Also in the Ara-maturi-no-miya[2]
   And in the Tuku-yomi-no-miya[32].   Thus I speak.

   The *kamu-nusi-be*[26] again respond: 'ôô.'

XX. GRAND SHRINE OF ISE: FESTIVAL OF THE DIVINE FIRST FRUITS BANQUET OF THE NINTH MONTH

(*Nagatuki no Kamu-nihe no maturi*)

By the solemn command of the Sovereign Grandchild[29],
I humbly speak in the solemn presence of Ama-terasi-masu-oho-mikami[1],
> Whose praises are fulfilled[24]
> On the upper reaches of the Isuzu river
> In Watarahi of Ise:

I humbly speak his solemn command
> Concerning the great offerings
>> Which are habitually presented at the Divine First-fruits
>> Banquet of the ninth month:

[To the effect that] prince (office, rank, name) and I (office, rank, name) of the Nakatomi[22], be sent as his messengers
> And that [the offerings] should be brought by the Imibe[16],
>> Having thick sashes over their weak shoulders,
> Be purified and presented. Thus I humbly speak.

XXI. GRAND SHRINE OF ISE: SAME FESTIVAL
AT TOYO-UKE-NO-MIYA

By the command of the Sovereign Grandchild[20],
I humbly speak before the Sovereign Deity[28]
    Whose praises are fulfilled[24]
    In the field of Yamada in Watarahi:

I humbly speak his great command
    Concerning the great offerings
        Which are habitually presented at the Divine First-fruits
        Banquet of the ninth month:
[To the effect that] prince (office, rank, name) and I (office, rank,
    name) of the Nakatomi[22], be sent as his messengers
    And that [the offerings] should be brought by the Imibe[16],
        Hanging thick sashes over their shoulders,
    Be purified and presented. Thus I humbly speak.

XXII. GRAND SHRINE OF ISE: SAME, DIVINE
FIRST FRUITS BANQUET
(*Kamu-nihe no maturi*)

All of you *kamu-nusi-be*[26] and *mono-imi*[26], hear the heavenly ritual,
  the solemn ritual words
    Which I humbly speak in the solemn presence of
      Ama-terasi-masu-sume-oho-mi-kami[1],
        Whose praises are fulfilled[24]
        With the great shrine posts firmly rooted
        And the cross-beams of the roof soaring high towards
          the High Heavenly Plain[15],
        On the upper reaches of the Isuzu river
        At Udi in Watarahi. Thus I speak.

      The *negi*[26] and *uti-bito*[26] together respond: 'ôô.'

By the solemn command of the Emperor[5],
[I pray] that you make his life a long life,
  Prospering [his reign] as an abundant reign,
  Eternal and unmoving as the sacred massed rocks,
That you favor also the princes which are born,
And that you guard, favor, and prosper long and tranquilly
  The various officials,
    As well as even the common people of the lands of the four
      quarters of the kingdom.
With this prayer [I offer]
    The great wine and the great first-fruits prepared in ritual purity
      Habitually presented by the people of the Kamube[19]
        Established in the three counties and in the various
          lands and various places
    As well as their tribute suspended,
      The thousand-fold and five-hundred-fold tribute,
  Placing these abundantly like a long mountain range.
I, the great Nakatomi[22], abiding concealed behind the solemn

tama-gusi[31],

On the seventeenth day of the ninth month of this year,

Do humbly praise you with the heavenly ritual, the solemn ritual words
    As the morning sun rises in effulgent glory.

Hear me, all of you *kamu-nusi-be*[26] and *mono-imi*[26]. Thus I speak.

The negi[26] and uti-bito[26] together respond: 'ôô.'

Say this and present them
    Also in the Ara-maturi-no-miya[2]
    And in the Tuku-yomi-no-miya[32]. Thus I speak.

The kamu-nusi-be[26] together respond: 'ôô.'

XXIII. GRAND SHRINE OF ISE: WHEN THE HIGH PRIESTESS ASSUMES HER OFFICE

(Ituki-no-hime-miko wo Ire-maturu toki)

After finishing speaking the words for presenting the offerings
  of the Divine First Fruits Banquet, the following is said:

I humbly speak in special words:
The Consecrated Princess[25] now being presented, has been,
  According to the ancient custom,
  Blessed and purified for three years
  And designated as your handmaiden
[With the prayer] that you do grant that the Sovereign Grandchild[29]
  may abide tranquilly and peacefully
  Together with the heaven and earth, with the sun and moon,
  Eternal and unmoving.
The great command to present her as your handmaiden
  Is relayed as an intermediary
    By the great Nakatomi[22],
    As if grasping an awesome spear in the middle,
  And fearfully and reverently spoken. Thus I humbly speak.

XXIV. GRAND SHRINE OF ISE: NORITO ON MOVING THE SHRINE OF THE GREAT DEITY

(Use also for the Toyo-uke-no-miya)

By the solemn command of the Sovereign Grandchild[29],
I humbly speak in the solemn presence of the Great Sovereign Deity[28]:

In accordance with the ancient custom,
    The great shrine is built anew once in twenty years,
The various articles of clothing of fifty-four types,
    And the sacred treasures of twenty-one types are provided,
And exorcism, purification, and cleansing is performed.

I, the functionary participating (rank, surname, name), have been
    dispatched
        To say the manner in which the offerings are to be presented.
        Thus I humbly speak.

XXV. TO DRIVE AWAY A VENGEFUL DEYTY
(*Tataru Kami wo Utusi-yaru*)

By the command of the Ancestral Gods and Goddesses[27],
    Who divinely remain in the High Heavenly Plain[15],
    And who began matters,
The eight myriad deities were convoked in a divine convocation
  in the high meeting-place of Heaven,
        And consulted in a divine consultation, [saying]:
            'Our Sovereign Grandchild[29] is to rule
            'The Land of the Plentiful Reed Plains and of
                the Fresh Ears of Grain[10]
            'Tranquilly as a peaceful land.'
Thus he left the heavenly rock-seat,
    And descended from the heavens,
        Pushing with an awesome pushing through the myriad layers
            of heavenly clouds
    And was entrusted [with the land]—
Then they consulted with a divine consultation, [saying]:
    'Which deity should first be dispatched
    'To expel with a divine expulsion and to pacify
    'The unruly deities in the Land of the Fresh Ears of Grain[10]?'
Then the numerous deities all consulted and said:
    'Ame-no-ho-hi-no-mikoto should be sent to pacify them.'
Then when he was dispatched down from the heavens,
    He did not return to report on his mission.
Next Take-mi-kuma-no-mikoto was also dispatched,
    But he also, obeying his father's words, did not return
        to report on his mission.
Again, Ame-waka-hiko was also dispatched,
    But he did not return to report on his mission,
    But because of woe from a bird of on high
    Immediately lost his life.
Hereupon by the command of the Heavenly Deities
    Another consultation was held,

And the two deities:
    Futu-nusi-no-mikoto
    And Take-mika-duti-no-mikoto
    Were caused to descend from the heavens;
They expelled with a divine expulsion the unruly deities
    And pacified with a divine pacification;
They silenced to the last leaf
    The rocks and the stumps of the trees,
    Which had been able to speak,
And when the Sovereign Grandchild[29] descended from the heavens,
    Entrusted [the land to him].

The lands of the four quarters thus entrusted [to him when he]
    descended from the heavens,
        Great Yamato, the land of the Sun-Seen-on-High, was determined
            as a peaceful land;
The palace posts were firmly rooted in the bed-rock below,
    The cross-beams of the roof soaring high towards the
        High Heavenly Plain[15],
    And [the palace of the Emperor] constructed as a heavenly
        shelter, as a sun-shelter[11]
    In this land which he is to rule tranquilly as a peaceful land.
May the Sovereign Deities[28] dwelling within the heavenly palace
    Not rage and not ravage,
Because as deities they are well acquainted
    With the matters begun in the High Heavenly Plain[15];
May they rectify [their hearts] in the manner of [the rectifying deities]
    Kamu-naho-bi and Oho-naho-bi,
And may they go from this place
    And move to another place of lovely mountains and rivers
        Where they can look out over the four quarters,
    And may they reign over that as their place.

With this prayer I present offerings,
    Providing garments of colored cloth, radiant cloth, plain cloth,
        and coarse cloth;

A mirror as something to see clearly with,
A jewel as something to play with,
A bow and arrow as something to shoot with,
A sword as something to cut with,
A horse as something to ride on;
Wine, raising high the soaring necks
    Of the countless wine vessels, filled to the brim;
In rice and in stalks;
That which lives in the mountains—
    The soft-furred and the coarse-furred animals—
That which grows in the vast fields and plains—
    The sweet herbs and the bitter herbs—
As well as that which lives in the blue ocean—
    The wide-finned and the narrow-finned fishes,
    The sea-weeds of the deep and the sea-weeds of the shore—
I place these noble offerings in abundance upon tables
    Like a long mountain range and present them
Praying that the Sovereign Deities[28]
    Will with a pure heart receive them tranquilly
        As offerings of ease,
        As offerings of abundance,
    And will not seek vengeance and not ravage,
But will move to a place of wide and lovely mountains and rivers,
    And will as deities dwell there pacified.
With this prayer, I fulfill your praises[24]. Thus I humbly speak.

XXVI. PRESENTING OFFERINGS ON DISPATCHING AN ENVOY TO CHINA

By the solemn command of the Sovereign Grandchild[29],
I humbly speak before you,
    The deities whose praises are fulfilled[24] in Sumi-no-ye:

Because there was no suitable port
    For dispatching envoys to China,
[The Emperor] was considering
    Having them board ship from the land of Harima.
Just then, a divine command came, instructing and teaching:
    'I will build a port.'
Exactly in accordance with this instruction and teaching,
    A port was built.
Whereupon [the Emperor] was glad and rejoiced
    And as tokens of reverence
      Had [me] (office, rank, surname, name) bring and present
      to you these offerings. Thus I humbly speak.

XXVII. DIVINE CONGRATULATORY WORDS OF THE KUNI-NO-MIYATUKO[20] OF IDUMO

(*Idumo no Kuni-no-miyatuko no Kamu-yogoto*)

Although there may be many days,
    Today, this day of life, this day of plenty
Is when I (surname, name), kuni-no-miyatuko[20] of Idumo,
    Fearfully and reverently do speak:

Awesome to mention is the incarnate deity
    Who rules the Great Eight-Island Land[9]
And whose reign is to be blessed
    As a long reign, a secure reign.

In the land of Idumo, fenced round about
    With a wall of green mountains,
The shrine posts are firmly planted in the bed-rock below,
    And the cross-beams of the roof soar high towards the
        High Heavenly Plain[15]:

At this shrine dwell two deities:
    The beloved offspring of Izanagi, the ancestral god[27],
    The great deity of Kumano, Kusi-mi-ke-no-no-mikoto;
    And the land-creator Oho-namoti-no-mikoto;

Which two deities, besides all the Sovereign Deities[28]
    Dwelling in the hundred and eighty-six shrines, [I worship]:
        Hanging thick sashes over my weak shoulders,
        Securing the cord of the sacred cloths
            Worn on the head as a heavenly head-gear,
        In the sacred abode mowing and spreading out
            Wild grasses as a sacred sitting-mat,
        Blackening well the sacred cooking vessels;
            And with the heavenly wine-distilling vats in peace,
    I do thus remain confined in ritual abstinence,

And do abstain and pacify [them] in the pacifying-shrine
And, as the morning sun rises in effulgent glory,
    Do humbly speak the congratulatory words of divine blessing
      As a report on this worship.
      Thus I humbly speak.

When the deities of High Heaven:
    Take-mi-musu-bi
    And Kamu-musu-bi-no-mikoto
    Entrusted to the rule of the Sovereign Grandchild[29]
      the Great Eight-Island Land[9],
    The distant ancestor of the omi[20] of Idumo,
      Ame-no-ho-hi-no-mikoto,
    Was dispatched to inspect the land.
Pushing through the myriad layers of heavenly clouds,
    Flying the heavens and flying the earth,
    He looked throughout the kingdom,
    And then reported on his search:
      'The Land of the Plentiful Reed Plains and of the Fresh
        Ears of Grain[10]
      'During the day seethes as with summer flies,
      'And during the night is overrun with gods which shine
        as sparks of fire.
      'The very rocks, the stumps of trees,
      'The bubbles of water all speak,
      'And it is truly an unruly land.
      'But I shall pacify and subjugate it,
      'And shall have it ruled tranquilly
      'By the Sovereign Grandchild[29] as a peaceful land.'
Thus saying, he dispatched his son
    Ame-no-hina-dori-no-mikoto,
      Together with Futu-nusi-no-mikoto,
    And caused them to descend from the heavens.
The two swept away and subjugated the unruly deities,
    Propitiated and pacified the great Land-creator,
    And caused him to relinquish the rule
      Of the visible, material things in the Great Eight-Island Land[9].

Then Oho-namoti-no-mikoto said:
    'The Sovereign Grandchild[29] will dwell peacefully in the
        land of Yamato.'
Thus saying, he attached his peaceful spirit
    To a mirror of large dimensions,
    Eulogizing it by the name
        Yamato-no-oho-mono-nusi-Kusi-mika-tama-no-mikoto,
    And had it dwell in the sacred grove of Oho-miwa.
He caused the spirit of his son
    Adi-suki-taka-hiko-ne-no-mikoto
    To dwell in the sacred grove of Kamo in Kaduraki;
Caused the spirit of Koto-siro-nusi-no-mikoto
    To dwell in Unade;
And caused the spirit of Kayanarumi-no-mikoto
    To dwell in the sacred grove of Asuka.
[These deities] he presented to the Sovereign Grandchild[29]
    As his close protector-deities,
And himself dwelt peacefully
    In the shrine of Kiduki of the myriad clay.
Then the Sovereign Ancestral Gods and Goddesses[27] said:
    'Do you, oh Ame-no-ho-hi-no-mikoto, bless the long reign,
        the great reign of the Emperor[5]
    'As eternal and unmoving,
    'And do you prosper it as an abundant reign.'
Thus do I, inheriting this tradition,
    Perform the worship service,
    And as the morning sun rises in effulgent glory
    Do present, as tokens of homage of the deities and as tokens of
        homage of the omi[20],
        The sacred treasures of blessing. Thus I humbly speak.

As the white jewels,
    May you abide with hoary hairs;
As the bright red jewels,
    May you abide with ruddy features;

As the blue jewels,
   Arranged in orderly strings of noble beads,
   May you rule as an incarnate deity
      The Great Eight-Island Land[9],
And may your long reign, your great reign
   Be as a broad-bladed sword, tempered and hardened well.
The prancing of the hooves of the fore-legs
   And of the hind-legs of the white horse
   Is to stamp firm the posts
      Of the inner and outer palace gates unto the upper rocks
   And to stamp them hard unto the bed-rock below;
The pricking up of its ears
   Is as a blessing of your rule.
As the white swans [presented] for your pleasure as a live tribute,
   And as the rustic striped cloth, may your heart be firm.
As the young ponds which spring up
   By this old river bank and that old river bank,
   May you always be young with an ever more exuberant youth.
As the waters [run] in the pool where purification ablutions are made,
   May you ever become younger with a continual rejuvenation.
In the manner of wiping clean and viewing
   The surface of a smooth, clear mirror,
   May you, the incarnate deity, rule [clearly] the Great Eight-Island
      Land[9]
      Together with heaven and earth, sun and moon,
      Peacefully and tranquilly; as a sign thereof
I bear the divine treasures of blessing
[And present them] as tokens of homage of the deities and tokens of
   homage of the omi[20],
   And fearfully and reverently,
   Do humbly speak the congratulatory words of divine blessing of
      heavenly tradition. Thus I humbly speak.

XXVIII. CONGRATULATORY WORDS OF THE NAKATOMI

(*Nakatomi no Yogoto*)

Before the Emperor Oho-yamato-neko[23],
    Who rules the Great Eight-Island Land[9] as an incarnate deity,
I [speak] the congratulatory words of the heavenly deities
    And fulfill his praises[24]. Thus I humbly speak.

By the command of the Sovereign Ancestral Gods and Goddesses[27],
    Who divinely remain in the High Heavenly Plain[15],
The eight myriad deities were convoked, [and the command given]:
    'From the beginning in the High Heavenly Plain[15],
    'The Sovereign Grandchild[29] is commanded to rule
    'The Land of the Plentiful Reed Plains and of the Fresh Ears
        of Grain[10]
    'Tranquilly as a peaceful land.
    'Abiding upon the heavenly high seat of the heavenly sun-lineage[14],
    'He is to partake tranquilly and peacefully in the sacred
        ceremonial place
    'Of the fresh ears of grain for a thousand autumns, for five
        hundred autumns
    'As his heavenly food, his eternal food, his everlasting food.'
Receiving this trust,
    He descended from the heavens.
After this, Ame-no-ko-yane-no-mikoto,
    The distant ancestor of the Nakatomi[22],
    Served before the Sovereign Grandchild[29],
And sent [his son] Ame-no-osi-kumo-ne-no-kami up to the heavenly
    double-peaked [mountain]
    And had him speak humbly before the Ancestral Gods and
        Goddesses[27] in order to receive [their words].
    He instructed him to speak humbly:
        'We wish to present to the Sovereign Grandchild[29] at his meals
        'Water of the visible lands, to which heavenly water has

been added.'
In accordance with this, Ame-no-osi-kumo-ne-no-kami, riding on a
heavenly floating cloud,
Went up to the heavenly double-peaked [mountain]
And spoke humbly before the Ancestral Gods and Goddesses[27].
Then they entrusted him with a heavenly jeweled comb [and
commanded]:
'Stand this jeweled comb up,
'And from the time that the waning sun goes down until the
morning sun shines
'Recite the heavenly ritual, the solemn ritual words.
'If you thus recite,
'As a sign, sacred manifold bamboo shoots will sprout forth
like young water plants,
'And from underneath many heavenly springs will gush forth.
'Take this water and have him partake of it as heavenly water.'
Thus it was entrusted.

In accordance with this trust, he partakes of the fresh ears of grain
in the sacred ceremonial place:
The diviners[3] of the four lands have divined by means of the grand
divination
And have ceremonially determined as the Yuki[34] [the county of]
Yasu in the land of Afumi
And as the Suki[34] [the county of] Higami in the land of Taniha.
Those in charge of the ceremonial paddy[7]:
The saka-tu-ko,
The saka-nami,
The ko-basiri,
The hahi-yaki,
The kamagi-kori,
The ahi-dukuri,
And the ina-no-mi-no-kimi
Have all [performed their duties] and brought [the rice] to the
sacred ceremonial place of the banquet of the first fruits.
Thus, on the second day of the Hare of the eleventh month of this year,

[The rice] has been solemnly and strictly,
Fearfully and reverently purified and presented,
And a day in the month chosen and determined
    For the great wine, the black wine and the white wine of the Yuki[34]
        and the Suki[34],
    To be consumed by the Emperor Yamato-neko[23]
        With a ruddy countenance
          As his heavenly food, his eternal food, his everlasting food,
        In liquor and in fruit,
    And for him to feast with ruddy countenance at the abundant
    banquet.

May the Sovereign Deities[28] also,
    Whose praises are fulfilled[24] with these congratulatory words of
        the Heavenly Deities,
    Concur together in this common first-fruit banquet of a thousand
        autumns and five hundred autumns,
    Bless him as unmoving and eternal,
    And cause [his reign] to flourish as an abundant reign;
And from this first year of Kōdi [1142]
    May he, together with heaven and earth, with the sun and
        the moon,
    Continue to give out light and radiance.
[With this prayer] as an intermediary,
    As if grasping—not the top or bottom—
        But the middle of an awesome spear,
    I, the Nakatomi[22] head-priest, Nakatomi no asomi Kiyotika,
    greater fourth court rank, higher official rank, assistant
    minister of the Office of Rites,
    Fulfill your praises[24] with congratulatory words.
    Thus I humbly speak.

Again I humbly speak:
    You princes of the blood, princes, court nobles, many officials,
        Who serve at the Emperor's[5] court,
    As well as the common people of the lands of the four quarters of

the kingdom,
Assemble all together and see,
Feel reverence,
Rejoice,
And hear.
May these words,
Praying that the Emperor's[5] court will flourish as an abundant reign, like luxuriant trees,
Be heard. Thus do I fearfully and reverently pray.
Thus I humbly speak.

XXIX. HOUSE-BLESSING FORMULA (Muro-hogi)
OF PRINCE WOKE

The ropes of the young *muro* house built up,
The pillars built up
    Are the mainstay of the heart of the lord of this house.
The beams laid in place
    Are the flourishing of the heart of the lord of this house.
The rafters laid in place
    Are the setting in order of the heart of the lord of this house.
The crosspieces laid in place
    Are the levelness of the heart of the lord of this house.
The ropes tied in place
    Are the firm securing of the life of the lord of this house.
The grass thatched on the roof
    Is the abundance of the wealth of the lord of this house.

Idumo is newly cultivated;
The rice ears, ten hands long, of the newly cultivated fields
    Have been distilled to wine in shallow vessels;
Partake thereof with pleasure,
    Oh my lads.

As I dance,
    Lifting up the horns
    Of a deer of these hills—
You cannot buy such as this
    In the market of Wega of the tasty wine!
So clap your hands heartily,
    My eternal ones!

XXX. WORDS SPOKEN BY KUSI-YA-TAMA-NO-KAMI

This fire which I drill—
    May it burn upwards
        Until, on the plentiful heavenly new lattice
           Of Kami-musu-bi-no-mi-oya-no-mikoto
           In the High Heavenly Plain
        The soot hangs down eight hands long;
    And until, under the ground,
        The bottom bed-rock is burned solid.
The fishermen fishing spread out the *taku* ropes,
    The thousand-fathom ropes;
    And, with a rustling, rustling sound,
        Draw hither and raise up the wide-mouthed, broad-finned
           perch.
Thus I will present the heavenly sea-food viands
    Until the very split-bamboo trays
    Bend down under the weight!

XXXI. BLESSING FORMULA OF MI-OYA-NO-
KAMI-NO-MIKOTO

How dear my descendants!
   How lofty the divine shrine!
Even with heaven and earth,
   Together with the sun and moon.
The people assemble in joy;
   Food and drink is abundant.
For all generations without end,
   Day by day ever more flourishing,
Until myriads of years hence
   The pleasure will not cease.

XXXII. WORDS SPOKEN BY ITODE

I, your humble servant, do present these offerings
    [With the prayer] that you may rule the land minutely
        As the curves of the large-dimensioned beads,
    That you may look upon the mountains, rivers, and the ocean
    clearly
        As the white copper mirror.
Take, therefore, this sword, ten hands long,
    And with it pacify the kingdom.

GLOSSARY

1 AMA-TERASU-OHO-MI-KAMI

Modern reading: Ama-terasu-ō-mi-kami.

Also: Ama-terasi-masu-sume-oho-mi-kami; Ama-terasi-masu-oho-mi-kami.

'Great Deity Illuminating the Heavens.' The Sun-Goddess worshipped at the Grand Shrine of Ise.

    I VII XVIII XX XXII

2 ARA-MATURI-NO-MIYA

Modern reading: Ara-matsuri-no-miya.

A subsidiary shrine within the precincts of the Grand Shrine of Ise where the *ara-mi-tama*, 'rough spirit' of the Sun-Goddess is enshrined. It is the first of the subsidiary shrines of Ise.

    XVIII XIX XXII

3 DIVINERS *urabe*

Urabe is the common title for those who practiced divination. In ancient times the diviners of the lands of Izu, Iki, and Tsushima were renowned; and the word Urabe was adopted by many as their surname. In the Norito, it is not clear which lands are meant by "diviners of the four lands."

In the Great Exorcism, it is the diviners who carry away the sin-bearing articles and cast them into the river. In the Congratulatory Words of the Nakatomi, it is they who determine by divination the ceremonial rice fields Yuki and Suki (q.v.). The Urabe clan pronounce the *norito* of the Fire-Pacifying Festival and the Miti-ahe no Maturi, and possibly that of the Great Exorcism.

    X XXVIII

4 EARTHLY SINS *kuni-tu-tumi*

Modern reading: kuni-tsu-tsumi.

The sins to be exorcised in the Great Exorcism are divided into Heavenly Sins *ama-tu-tumi* (q.v.) and Earthly Sins *kuni-tu-tumi*. The earthly sins enumerated here seem to include a number which we would identify as 'pollutions,' such as skin diseases, impurities emanating from insects, etc., as well as forbidden sexual relations.

(cf. Kaneko, *Engi-shiki Norito Kō,* p. 446-459)

X

5 EMPEROR *Sumera*

The Emperor is referred to as either *Sumera* or as *Sume-mi-ma-no-mikoto* (Sovereign Grandchild, q.v.). *Sumera* is related etymologically with the element *sume.* See SOVEREIGN ANCESTRAL GODS AND GODDESSES.

II V VI X XV XVI XVII XXII XXVII XXVIII

6 FIVE TYPES OF THINGS *itu-iro no mono*

Modern reading: itsu-iro no mono.

Traditionally regarded as meaning 'thin coarse-silk of five colors.' Other interpretations are 'the five sacred treasures.' Kaneko reads as *ikusa no mono* and interprets as meaning 'weapons.' (cf. Kaneko, *Engi-shiki Norito Kō,* p. 371-375)

III XII XV

7 FUNCTIONARIES OF THE CEREMONIAL PADDY

In the Congratulatory Words of the Nakatomi, the following offices are mentioned in connection with the Yuki and Suki ceremonial paddies (see YUKI AND SUKI):

a. Saka-tu-ko—a virgin who played the most important role in ceremonial rice production; her main duty was to distill the black wine and the white wine.

b. Saka-nami—a woman who served as assistant to the Saka-tu-ko.

c. Ko-basiri—a woman whose duty was sifting.

d. Hahi-yaki—literally 'ash-burner;' a man whose duty was to make the ash preparation used to flavor the black wine and the white wine.

e. Kamagi-kori—four men who served as wood-cutters, gathering fuel to prepare the first fruits.

f. Ahi-dukuri—two women assistants who helped in distilling the wine.

g. Ina-no-mi-no-kami—a man porter whose duty was to carry the rice stalks.

XXVIII

8 GRAIN DEITIES *Mi-tosi no sume-gami-tati*

Modern reading: Mi-toshi no sume-gami-tachi.

The Sovereign Deities of the Grain seem to include all those deities who are in charge of the grain crop. The word *tosi*, which means 'year' in modern Japanese, here means 'grain,' particularly 'rice.'
  I

9 GREAT EIGHT-ISLAND LAND *Oho-yasima-guni*

Modern reading: Ō-yashima-guni.

According to the Kojiki and Nihon Shoki, the eight major Japanese islands created by the godly couple Izanagi and Izanami; therefore, the land of Japan. (see also ISLANDS.)
  IV XXVII XXVIII

10 GREAT EIGHT-ISLAND LAND OF THE PLENTIFUL REED PLAINS AND OF THE FRESH EARS OF GRAIN *Oho-yasima Toyo-asi-hara no Midu-ho no kuni*

Also: Land of the Plentiful Reed Plains and of the Fresh Ears of Grain *Toyo-asi-hara no Midu-ho no kuni*; Land of the Fresh Ears of Grain *Midu-ho no kuni*.

Modern reading: Ō-yashima Toyo-ashi-hara no Mizu-ho no kuni.

Eulogistic names for Japan. They appear also in the mythological sections of the Kojiki.
  VIII X XII XXV XXVII XXVIII

GREAT NAKATOMI—see NAKATOMI

GREAT SOVEREIGN DEITY—see SOVEREIGN DEITY

11 HEAVENLY SHELTER, SUN-SHELTER *ame no mi-kage, hi no mi-kage*

A phrase frequently applied to a palace or shrine in which the Emperor or a deity is said to dwell. There have been many theories about its meaning:
  a. 'a building covering the heavens, a building covering the sun.'
  b. 'a shelter from the rain, a shelter from the sun.'
  c. 'a place receiving the heavenly rays, the rays of the sun.'
  Satow translates as: 'a shade from the heavens, a shade from the sun.'

I follow Kaneko in interpreting *ame no* and *hi no* as being eulogisms having no essential semantic relation to the word *mi-kage,* which means 'shade,' 'shelter,' 'ray,' 'shadow.' Both *ame no* and *hi no* have lost their original meanings and are used as formalized eulogistic modifiers. (cf. Kaneko, *Engi-shiki Norito Kō,* p. 356-361)

I II V VIII X XV XXV

12 HEAVENLY SHRINES, EARTHLY SHRINES *Ama-tu-yasiro kuni-tu-yasiro*

Modern reading: Ama-tsu-yashiro kuni-tsu-yashiro.

An expression meaning the sum total of all shrines which received government support. The term seems often to be used in the sense of 'the deities enshrined in the Heavenly Shrines and Earthly Shrines' —in other words, the enshrined deity and the shrine wherein enshrined were verbally confused.

The elements *ama-tu* 'heavenly' and *kuni-tu* 'earthly' are also found in the parallel phrases *ama-tu-kami* 'heavenly deities' and *kuni-tu-kami* 'earthly deities'; for this reason, the traditional interpretation has been: 'shrines wherein are enshrined heavenly deities and earthly deities.' Kaneko holds that in this case the elements *ama-tu* and *kuni-tu* are merely formal modifiers having no essential semantic relation to the word *yasiro* 'shrine'. (cf. Kaneko, *Engi-shiki Norito Kō,* p. 330-333)

I IV VII XIV

13 HEAVENLY SINS *ama-tu-tumi*

Modern reading: ama-tsu-tsumi.

The sins to be exorcised in the Great Exorcism are divided into Heavenly Sins *ama-tu-tumi* and Earthly Sins *kuni-tu-tumi* (q.v.) A similarity between the heavenly sins enumerated in the *norito* for the Great Exorcism and the various misdemeanors perpetrated by the god Susa-no-wo in Heaven has been noted; and the connection of these Heavenly Sins with agriculture has also been frequently remarked upon. A fairly new theory advanced by Kaneko is that the Heavenly Sins include many—such as causing ritual impurity by defecation—which are black magic practices. (cf. Kaneko, *Engi-shiki Norito Kō,* p. 446-459)

X

14 HEAVENLY SUN-LINEAGE *ama-tu-hi-tugi*

Modern reading: ama-tsu-hi-tsugi.

Eulogism for the Imperial lineage. Kaneko regards *ama-tu* and *hi* as mere formal modifiers having no essential semantic relation with *tugi* 'succession,' 'lineage.' (cf. Kaneko, *Engi-shiki Norito Kō*, p. 403-407)

VIII XXVIII

15 HIGH HEAVENLY PLAIN *Takama-no-hara*

The abode of the heavenly deities as distinguished from the visible world of men. "In Shinto, *ame* or Heaven is a lofty, sacred world, the home and dwelling place of the *Ama-tsu-kami* or Heavenly Gods. The word *Takama no Hara* is used eulogistically of it...*Takama no Hara* is the Upper World in a religious sense." *Basic Terms of Shinto*, p. 68.

I II V VI VII VIII X XII XIII XV XVIII XXII XXV XXVII XXVIII

16 IMIBE

Modern reading: Imube, Imbe.

One of the clan groups called *be* which in the ancient social system served the Court by practicing a definite occupation. This clan, dwelling in various localities throughout the country, practiced ritual abstinence (*imi, mono-imi*) and was in charge of preparing offerings and ritual paraphernalia and offering them to the deities.

These local clans were ruled by the Imibe clan (*uzi*), the family, claiming descent from the deity Ame-no-futo-tama-no-mikoto, which was in charge of making offerings in the Yamato Court—while the Nakatomi clan (q.v.) was in charge of reciting the *norito*. In the early ninth century AD the Imibe family was eclipsed by the Nakatomi family.

The Engi-shiki states that the *norito* of the Blessing of the Great Palace (VIII) and the Festival of the Gates (IX) were recited by the Imibe clan, and they figure also in various other *norito*.

I VII VIII XIV XX XXI

17 IMPERIAL PLANTATIONS *mi-agata*

Lands in the Home Provinces belonging directly to the Imperial Court,

where food for the Emperor's table was grown. There were six of
them in these ancient locations: Taketi, Kaduraki, Tohoti, Siki,
Yamanobe, and Sofu. The head of the plantation was called
agata-nusi. Later, these plantations were established throughout the
country. Each plantation was protected by a tutelary deity which
was worshipped at different occasions throughout the year.

I III IV VII

18 ISLANDS *sima*

Modern reading: shima.

Although in modern Japanese *shima* means 'island,' anciently the word
was more or less synonymous with *kuni* 'land.' Thus *sima* in the
norito may always refer to a region or district, one not necessarily
bounded by water. However, I have consistently translated the
word here as 'island.'

I VII XII

19 KAMUBE

Modern reading: Kambe, Kōbe.

Groups of peasantry attached to certain lands the income of which
was devoted to the support of a shrine.

XIX XXII

20 KUNI-NO-MIYATUKO

A title given to local rulers in the political system before the Taika
Reform (645 AD). Some of these local rulers were the hereditary
rulers of formerly independent regions which became possessions
of the Yamato Court, while others were appointed and sent out by
the central government.

The word literally means 'ruler of a land,' but the land *kuni* which
they ruled was not as large as the *kuni* in the later administrative
system, but corresponded more to the subsequent *kohori* 'county.' .

The *kuni-no-miyatuko* of Idumo, after the Taika Reform, devoted themselves largely to religious matters. In the Divine Congratulatory
Words of the Kuni-no-miyatuko of Idumo (XXVII) the *kuni-no-
miyatuko* refers to himself as the *omi* of Idumo: *omi* was at this
time a hereditary rank, while *kuni-no-miyatuko* was then a ceremonial office.

XXVII

LAND OF THE PLENTIFUL REED PLAINS AND OF THE FRESH EARS OF GRAIN—see GREAT EIGHT-ISLAND LAND OF THE PLENTIFUL REED PLAINS AND OF THE FRESH EARS OF GRAIN.

21 MOUNTAIN ENTRANCES *yama-no-kuti*

Modern reading: yama-no-kuchi.

Worship was paid to the deities of the Mountain Entrances of six mountains in the Yamato area: Asuka, Ihara, Osaka, Hatuse, Unebi, and Miminasi. The lumber used in palace construction was traditionally cut from these mountains.

I III VII

22 NAKATOMI

An ancient family, claiming descent from the deity Ame-no-ko-yane-no-mikoto, which served the Yamato Court in a priestly capacity together with the rival Imibe family (q.v.). Their duties were to recite the *norito*, and the Engi-shiki states—mistakenly—that all the *norito* in volume 8 except the two (VIII and IX) recited by the Imibe, were recited by the Nakatomi. In the early ninth century a quarrel developed between the Nakatomi and the Imibe, and the Nakatomi eventually won supremacy.

The Great Nakatomi *Oho-Nakatomi* evidently refers to the member of the family who officiated at ritual functions; thus it was no doubt the name of an office held by a single individual of the family rather than a family title.

X XIX XX XXI XXIII XXVIII

23 OHO-YAMATO-NEKO

Modern reading: Ō-yamato-neko.

Also: *Yamato-neko*.

A title belonging to the Emperor, meaning 'ruler of Great Yamato.' Does not necessarily refer to any one Emperor.

XXVIII

PLANTATIONS—see IMPERIAL PLANTATIONS.

24 PRAISES ARE FULFILLED *tatahe-goto wohe-maturu*

Modern reading: tatae-goto oe-matsuru.

A *norito* stock phrase, meaning literally, 'to complete, to exhaust the words of praise.' Used in various contexts to mean: 'to praise to the full,' 'to fulfill all the requirements of worship of,' 'to present to.'

25 PRIESTESSES

Usually *mi-kamunagi, kamunagi*. Women who serve the deities, more modernly called *miko*. The word *kamunagi* is believed to be derived from *kamu* 'deity' plus *nagi* 'pacification,' i.e., one who pacifies a deity. Various types are mentioned in the *norito*:

a. *oho-mi-kamunagi* 'High Priestess.' She was in charge of the worship of the eight protecting deities within the Imperial Court: Kami-musu-bi, Taka-mi-musu-bi, Iku-musu-bi, Taru-musu-bi, Tama-tume-musu-bi, Oho-miya-no-me, Oho-mi-ke-tu-kami, and Koto-siro-nusi.
   I VII

b. *Wigasuri no mi-kamunagi* 'Priestess of Wigasuri.' This priestess worshipped the deities who protected the land where the Palace was located: Iku-wi, Saku-wi, Tu-naga-wi, Asuha, and Hahiki.
   I VII

c. *Mi-kado no mi-kamunagi* 'Priestess of the Gates.' This priestess worshipped the protecting deities of the entrances to the Imperial Palace: Kusi-iha-mato-no-mikoto and Toyo-iha-mato-no-mikoto.
   I VII

d. *Iku-sima no mi-kamunagi* 'Priestess of Iku-sima.' The priestess who worshipped the deities of Iku-sima, the spirits of the entire land of Japan: Iku-kuni and Taru-kuni.
   I VII

e. *Ituki-no-hime-miko* 'The Consecrated Princess.' A virgin princess of the blood selected to serve as the High Priestess of the Grand Shrine of Ise. Her term of office lasted as long as the reign of the Emperor, and she retired at the end of the reign. She was purified by special rites for three years before going to assume her office in Ise.
   XXIII

26 PRIESTS

Various types of priests appear in the *norito*:

a. *kamu-dukasa* 'priest.' Appears only in the Miti-ahe no maturi and is believed to refer to the member of the Urabe (see

DIVINERS) family who was in charge of reciting this *norito*.
XIII

b. *kamu-nusi* (modern reading: kannushi) The person responsible
    for performing a certain ceremony of worship. "Literally, the
    head of those who serve a deity; one who, ranking above the
    negi and the *hafuri*, was in charge of everything concerned with
    divine worship." Tsugita, *Norito Shinkō*, p. 58. In early times
    kamu-nusi was not, as later, the name of a professional class of
    priests.
    I II III IV V VI VII XIV

c. *kamu-nusi-be. be* is a clan of persons sharing the same occupa-
    tion. Here, the priestly clan or class. Believed to be inclusive
    of *negi* and *uti-bito*.
    XIX XXII

d. *hafuri* A professional class of priests. Etymology unclear;
    variously interpreted as 'slaughterers,' 'those who bury the dead,'
    'prophets,' 'sleeve-flutterers,' 'exorcists.' The first two seem most
    plausible.
    I III IV VII XIV

e. *mono-imi* Virgins—including some boys—remaining in a state
    of ritual abstinence (*imi*) who served the Sun-Goddess at Ise.
    XIX XXII

f. *negi* A priestly rank in the Grand Shrine of Ise. Ranks above
    uti-bito.
    XVIII XIX XXII

g. *uti-bito* (modern reading: uchindo) A priestly rank in the
    Grand Shrine of Ise. Ranks below *negi*.
    XVIII XIX XXII

See also NAKATOMI, IMIBE, DIVINERS.

SIX PLANTATIONS—see IMPERIAL PLANTATIONS.

27 SOVEREIGN ANCESTRAL GODS AND GODDESSES *sume-*
    mutu-kamurogi kamuromi

Modern reading: sume-mutsu-kamurogi kamuromi.
Also: Ancestral Gods and Goddesses *mutu-kamurogi kamuromi*.
A term denoting two or more deities of the highest rank, often corresponding with Taka-mi-musu-bi and Ama-terasu-oho-mi-kami, the
ancestors of the Imperial House. In XXVII *kaburogi* 'the ancestral

god' is applied to Kusi-mi-ke-no-no-mikoto (i.e., Susa-no-wo-no-mikoto).

The element *sume* or *sube,* written with the Chinese character 皇, 'Imperial,' has been traditionally interpreted as connected with the verb *suberu* 'to rule,' 'to reign'; thus the usual English rendering as 'sovereign,' 'sovran.' Kaneko accepts Motowori's theory that *sume* is merely an honorific and is not necessarily connected with ruling or reigning. (cf. Kaneko, *Engi-shiki Norito Kō,* p. 318-319)

The element *mutu* (modern reading: mutsu) is generally agreed to mean 'affectionate,' 'akin,' 'related,' therefore 'ancestral.' It is connected with modern Japanese *mutsumajii* 'harmonious,' 'intimate,' 'friendly.'

The elements *kamurogi kamuromi* are less clear etymologically. *kamu* is generally regarded as equivalent to the word *kami* 'deity', and the endings *-gi* and *-mi* are usually endings denoting, respectively, masculine and feminine, as in *Izanagi* and *Izanami*. *ro* is regarded as a word-building particle without independent meaning.

Kaneko agrees with Motowori in reading this term *sumera ga mutu-kamurogi kamuromi* 'The Emperor's ancestral gods and goddesses' instead of the more frequent *sume-mutu-kamurogi kamuromi* 'sovereign ancestral gods and goddesses.'

See also EMPEROR *Sumera.*

I VII VIII X XII XIV XV XXV XXVII XXVIII

SOVEREIGN DEITIES OF THE GRAIN—see GRAIN DEITIES

28 SOVEREIGN DEITY *sume-gami*

Also: Great Sovereign Deity *sume-oho-mi-kami.*

A eulogistic term applied to various deities.

For the meaning of the element *sume* 'sovereign' see SOVEREIGN ANCESTRAL GODS AND GODDESSES.

I II III IV V VI VII XIII XIV XVI XXI XXV XXVIII

29 SOVEREIGN GRANDCHILD *sume-mi-ma-no-mikoto*

A term referring to the Emperor. Originally applied to the god Hiko-ho-no-ninigi-no-mikoto (or Ninigi-no-mikoto), the ancestor of the Imperial House. Emphasizes the lineal descendancy of the Emperor from his ancestors the Heavenly Deities.

For the meaning of the element *sume* 'sovereign' see SOVEREIGN

ANCESTRAL GODS AND GODDESSES.
See also EMPEROR *Sumera*.
I III IV VII VIII X XII XIII XIV XV XX XXI XXIII
XXIV XXV XXVI XXVII XXVIII

30 THE SOVEREIGN GRANDCHILD WHO RULED THE GREAT EIGHT-ISLAND LAND IN SIKISIMA *Sikisima ni Oho-yasima-guni sirosisi sume-mi-ma-no-mikoto*

Traditionally believed to refer to Emperor Sujin (traditional dates of reign 97-30 BC), who is said to have had his palace in Siki (a place in present Nara prefecture). However, Emperor Kimmei (traditional dates of reign 539-571 AD) also reigned in a place called Sikisima. Kaneko regards Sikisima as meaning Yamato as a whole, and says that no particular single Emperor is referred to here. (cf. Kaneko, *Engi-shiki Norito Kō*, p. 386-391)
IV

SUMERA—see EMPEROR

31 TAMA-GUSI

Modern reading: tama-gushi.

A type of sacred implement held by an officiant. It consisted of a branch or sprig of a sacred tree to which strips of *yufu* (modern reading: yū) cloth (or modernly, strips of paper) have been attached. In modern days *tama-gusi* are offered when formal worship is paid to a deity, or preserved as amulets to which the spirit of a deity is expected to attach itself.

Here the phrase is *futo-tama-gusi* 'solemn tama-gusi.'
XIX XXII

32 TUKU-YOMI-NO-MIYA

Modern reading: Tsuku-yomi-no-mıya.

A subsidiary shrine within the precincts of the Grand Shrine of Ise where the Moon Deity Tuku-yomi-no-mikoto is enshrined.
XIX XXII

URABE—see DIVINERS

33 WATER-PARTINGS *mi-kumari*

Believed to refer to the water-shed, the peak where the waters divide.

The deities of these peaks were worshipped as the tutelary deities of irrigation. Four mountain regions are mentioned as places of worship: Yosino, Uda, Tuke, and Kaduraki.

I VII

YAMATO-NEKO—see OHO-YAMATO-NEKO

34 YUKI AND SUKI

The regions chosen by divination for growing the rice to be used as sacred offerings in the Great First-fruits Festival.

See FUNCTIONARIES OF THE CEREMONIAL PADDY.

XXVIII